ROUTLEDGE 1
THE ECONOMICS
AN

Volume 3

OIL IN THE WORLD ECONOMY

OIL IN THE WORLD ECONOMY

Edited by
R. W. FERRIER AND A. FURSENKO

LONDON AND NEW YORK

First published in 1989 by Routledge

This edition first published in 2016
by Routledge
2 Park Square, Milton Park, Abingdon, Oxon OX14 4RN

and by Routledge
711 Third Avenue, New York, NY 10017

Routledge is an imprint of the Taylor & Francis Group, an informa business

British Library Cataloguing in Publication Data
A catalogue record for this book is available from the British Library

ISBN: 978-1-138-64127-3 (Set)
ISBN: 978-1-315-62232-3 (Set) (ebk)
ISBN: 978-1-138-64845-6 (Volume 3) (hbk)
ISBN: 978-1-138-64852-4 (Volume 3) (pbk)
ISBN: 978-1-315-62642-0 (Volume 3) (ebk)

Publisher's Note
The publisher has gone to great lengths to ensure the quality of this reprint but
points out that some imperfections in the original copies may be apparent.

Disclaimer
The publisher has made every effort to trace copyright holders and would welcome
correspondence from those they have been unable to trace.

Oil in the World Economy

Edited by

R. W. Ferrier

and

A. Fursenko

ROUTLEDGE
London and New York

First published 1989
by Routledge
11 New Fetter Lane, London EC4P 4EE
29 West 35th Street, New York NY 10001

Typeset by Pat and Anne Murphy, Highcliffe-on-Sea, Dorset
Printed and bound in Great Britain by Mackays of Chatham PLC, Kent

British Library Cataloguing in Publication Data

Oil in the world economy
  1. Petroleum industries and trades.
International economic aspects
I. Ferrier, R. W. II. Fursenko, A.
338.2'7282

  ISBN 0-415-00379-2

Library of Congress Cataloging in Publication Data

Oil in the world economy / edited by R. W. Ferrier and A. Fursenko.
  p.   cm.
  "Papers from . . . Ninth International Economic History
Congress of the Session B 'Oil in the World Economy'."
  ISBN 0-415-00379-2
  1. Petroleum industry and trade — History — 20th century —
Congresses. 2. Economic history — 20th century — Congresses.
I. Ferrier, R. W. (Ronald W.) II. Fursenko, A. A. III. International
Congress of Economic History (9th : 1986 : Berne, Switzerland).
Session B "Oil in the World Economy".
HD9560.5.O366 1989
338.2'7282'0904—dc20
89-32098 CIP

Contents

Contents

Tables and figures

Editors and contributors

Dr R. W. Ferrier
Formerly group historian, the British Petroleum Company

Dr Alexander Fursenko
Institute of History of the USSR, Leningrad

Professor Edith Penrose
Emeritus Professor, University of London (SOAS) and of
INSEAD (France)

Dr N. Ghorban
Mid-Continental Bank and Trust (W1), London

Mircea Buescu
Catholic University, Rio de Janeiro, Brazil

Dr R. Andreasjan
Institute of Oriental Studies, USSR

Jeffry A. Frieden
Department of Political Science, University of California,
Los Angeles

Professor V. A. Shishkin
Institute of History of the USSR, Leningrad

Alan L. Olmstead
Director of the Institute of Governmental Affairs,
University of California at Davis

Editors and contributors

Paul Rhode
A research associate at the Institute of Governmental Affairs,
University of California at Davis, and a graduate student in the
Department of Economics at Stanford University

Helmut Mejcher
Department of History, University of Hamburg

Professor Philippe Marguerat
University of Neuchatel, Switzerland

Hiroaki Fukami
Professor of Economics at Keio University, Tokyo

Introduction

These chapters originally formed part of the programme of the Ninth International Economic History Congress in Berne, August 1986, for one of the sessions, 'Oil in the world economy 1900–73', which was organized by the present editors. This occasion was the first time that the oil industry had featured on the agenda of the International Economic History Congress. Given the constraints of time and the scope of the subject it was inevitable that the choice of issues would be selective. It is recognized that this attitude may seem to some to be arbitrary in content and approach, but the lively discussion which followed the presentation of the papers indicates that it was very well received.

The programme was divided into two parts, that with a wide international perspective and that primarily national in emphasis. It is hoped that these collaborative studies will prove stimulating and provoke further consideration of the impact of oil in the world economy in its various aspects, so as to reach a more rational understanding of its impact of individual nations. We are not prescribing cures for balances between supply and demand and we are not making judgements on political factors, which have influenced important negotiations at various times. We are, however, commending a serious comparative attempt to appreciate the economic consequences of oil in the twentieth century as much as the earlier effects of the trade in and uses of precious and base metals, salt, spices, cereals, textiles, dyes, coal, chemicals and other significant commodities and natural resources.

By any standards the volume and value of world trade in oil is impressive. At the end of our period in 1973, the volume of trade moved by sea was 1,695 million tons. World oil production in the same year was 2,837.4 million tons and consumption 2,765.9 million tons. Compared with a production of 20,545,000 tons in 1900, this represents an enormous expansion. Oil reserves in the same year were 86,000 million tons. The part played by oil in an energy demand of 5,705.3 million tons of coal equivalent was 48.47 per cent. Estimates for oil investment were \$29.995 million, quadrupling in a decade to \$139,425 in 1982. The volume of shipping engaged in the oil trade was 220 million tons dw. Refinery capacity was 3,210 million tons.

In 1914, for example, the science of petroleum was rudimentary, just a simple analysis of its constituents and physical characteristics useful for the ordinary products of kerosine, benzine (motor spirit or gasoline) and fuel oil. Today an extraordinary range of specialized products is refined and a new industry of petrochemicals has facilitated our way of life particularly in household consumer goods. Transportation on earth and in space has been revolutionized and personal mobility in many parts of the world has been increased at an extraordinary rate. Admittedly, this has not been socially acceptable everywhere to the same extent, but within this century the horse and the camel have been replaced to a greater or lesser degree in most parts of the world. The possession of and the acquisition and financing of such resources have caused tension not only on economic grounds but also for political and strategic reasons, which cannot be ignored.

The chapters which follow attempt to illustrate on a selective and comparative basis, some of the problems of the oil industry: in exporting and importing; acquiring and defending interests; crises of scarcity and overproduction; funding, organizing and operating oil companies; the activities of national oil companies; governmental policies; commercial priorities and differing regional responses.

The editors are grateful to the contributing scholars for the research they have undertaken, the presentations which they have made and their friendly and international collaboration which has made this publication possible. We would like to pay our respects to the memory of Professor R. Andreasjan of the Union of Socialist Soviet Republics whose untimely and regrettable death, after completing his contribution, prevented him from attending the Congress.

Session one

Global aspects

Chapter one

Oil and the international economy: multinational aspects 1900–73

Professor Edith Penrose, Emeritus Professor, University of London (SOAS) and of INSEAD (France)

The oil resources of the world are unevenly distributed over the earth's surface and the concentration of reserves is not geographically coincident with the concentration of consumption. It was inevitable, therefore, that the industry would become internationally orientated and dominated by international trade, which would assume greater importance as the uses of oil in manufacturing and transport expanded and as industrial development spread throughout the world.

Of equal importance for the internationalization of the industry was the fact that the capital, technical and manpower resources required to discover and develop reserves were, at the dawn of the 'modern' age of oil in the middle of the Nineteenth century, also very unequally distributed among the countries of the world and, again, were geographically unmatched with the distribution of potential oil reserves. Thus the physical development of the world's oil resources required the international movement of capital and specialized skills.

Although south-east Asia and southern Europe, including Russia, were important oil producers in the latter part of the Nineteenth century, their resources were not only more limited than those of the United States but had been developed with foreign capital and foreign technology, in part American. Of the countries with extensive oil reserves only the United States was substantially industrialized, possessing within its own borders the capital, the skills, the technology and the organizing capacity required to exploit them successfully. With these advantages and a large domestic market, the United States soon became pre-eminent in the modern technology of drilling and refining, and quickly became the world's largest exporter of oil products. Except for a brief period towards the end of the century, it remained so until the Second World War.[1]

The United States was also perhaps the world's most advanced country with respect to large-scale business organization, and its large oil companies were capable of following up their success in export markets, not only with the successful acquisition of foreign crude oil resources to serve their foreign product markets, but also with the construction of refineries, transport and distribution systems. Five of the seven companies now known as the international 'majors' are American companies whose origins go back into this period of American oil history.[2]

The other two, British Petroleum and Royal Dutch/Shell, also originated in industrial countries but had, from the beginning, to build on oil resources developed far from home.[3] These countries, too, were capable of exporting the capital, skills and technology necessary to establish production, refining and distribution abroad. As industrial countries they not only possessed managerial capacity but also, and of great importance, a scientific approach to the solution of practical industrial problems, including, for the petroleum industry, the development of new uses for petroleum, improved refining technology and new markets for oil products.

It was the *integration*[4] of all stages in the physical process of production with the administrative framework of the few corporate groups dominating the world's oil industry outside the United States and the Soviet Union that moulded the industry into its truly multinational form. Each of these groups organized and administered all levels of the industry, integrating the upstream and the downstream activities through a large number of subsidiary companies, with holdings and directorships often shared with other companies, and operating across the boundaries of a large proportion of the countries of the world.

The so-called 'upstream' stages of the industry begin with the process of exploration and discovery, the location of which is confined to areas in which oil is expected, or hoped, to be found. The risk of disappointment is high. Once discovered, fields have to be delineated and developed to the point of production, but the timing of this and the extent to which it is carried depends in part on the way in which the 'owner' of the fields views the commercial prospects of production. The final upstream stage is the production of the crude oil and its transportation to gathering centres for immediate use in refineries or for shipment by trunk pipelines or tankers. Since crude oil is rarely used directly, the next stage downstream is a manufacturing operation – refining into products that can then be distributed directly to household or industrial consumers.[5]

In addition to the 'vertical' integration as described above, the oil groups are also horizontally integrated to a considerable

4

extent – that is, geographically integrated at any given level of production. For example, a group that owns crude oil production facilities (or refineries) in different countries, is horizontally integrated at the level of crude oil production (or refining); similarly for any other stage of the industry.

As a result of these types of integration, particularly the former, neither the international economic relationships within the industry nor the trade in crude oil were substantially at 'arm's length' until the fourth quarter of the Twentieth century. Nor were the flows of capital, technology and skills. They were rather flows administered in accordance with the plans and strategies of a very few large groups of companies. The fact that 'administration' was often ineffective and plans frustrated does not alter the main outlines of the structure or its functioning. The administration of each group and its competitive strategies affected not only the location, timing and speed at which reserves were discovered and developed throughout the world, but also the pattern of transport routes, the location of refining, the extension of distribution systems, and in consequence of all this, the flow and distribution of investment funds. Similarly, the policies of companies influenced the structure and level of prices and government revenues.

The emergence of the international structure

The international majors are Exxon (originally Standard Oil Company (New Jersey), here sometimes referred to as Standard Oil or Jersey Standard), Chevron (originally Standard Oil of California), Mobil (originally Socony), Gulf Oil, Texaco, British Petroleum (originally Anglo-Persian) and Royal Dutch/Shell (originally two companies, Shell Transport and Trading and Royal Dutch Petroleum Company). The first five are American companies and the first three were among the companies of the Standard Oil Trust which was broken up under the United States antitrust laws of 1911.[6] As a result of the antitrust decision, thirty-three of its subsidiaries became legally separate and independent companies. These included most of the companies responsible for its crude oil production and its transport facilities and for selling its products in the United Kingdom and the Far East. Jersey Standard retained its domestic and other European marketing subsidiaries but lacked its own sources of crude oil. In 1918 its net crude production was only about 16 per cent of the crude used in its refineries.

One of the companies that had been split off from the Standard Oil Trust was the Standard Oil Company of New York (Socony, now Mobil) which had been responsible for the Far Eastern marketing of Standard's products. Although Socony had a few refineries and also large marketing outlets in the Far East and the north-eastern United States, it had no crude oil production. Both Jersey Standard and Socony had strong incentives to acquire additional sources of crude oil, especially for their foreign operations.[7]

Numerous other American companies were also exploring for and developing oil resources abroad. Fears that reserves of oil in the United States were becoming severely diminished became widespread, especially in the 1920s, while at the same time there was a growing concern among companies and in the government that foreign groups, notably Shell and Anglo-Persian, were in the process of gaining monopoly control over the important oil resources outside the United States. Many of the newcomers failed to stay the course for a variety of reasons, including inadequate supplies of capital and an unwillingness to accept the risks and difficulties of operating in environments very different from those in the United States, and preferred to sell out to one or other of the majors. Jersey Standard, for example, acquired most of its main sources of crude outside the United States before the war through purchase and not discovery.

Among the companies that succeeded in establishing themselves abroad were Gulf Oil, which had found oil in Mexico and, in the 1920s, in Venezuela, and Standard Oil of California (an original member of the old Standard Oil Trust group of companies) whose really large discoveries of foreign oil came in the 1930s in Saudi Arabia and in Bahrain. Texaco entered the club of the majors through the purchase from Standard Oil of California of a half-interest in the Saudi and Bahraini concessions and of a concession in the Netherlands East Indies, for both of which it paid partly in cash and partly through an exchange for a half-interest in its marketing facilities in the Netherlands East Indies. Standard of California and Texaco formed the jointly-owned California-Texas Oil Company (Caltex), in the beginning to conduct their marketing operations, but Caltex quickly expanded at all stages of the industry throughout the Eastern Hemisphere operating on behalf of its two parents. Mobil and Exxon also obtained shares in the Saudi concession, completing its four-company American ownership.[8]

Royal Dutch/Shell and British Petroleum started out in different ways: Shell had its roots in the marketing of kerosene in the Far East and Europe in the last decades of the Nineteenth century, using oil from Baku.[9] Competition in European markets between

Shell and other interests based on Baku oil on the one hand, and Standard Oil on the other, and in the Far East among these groups plus the Royal Dutch, was intense. Numerous successful and unsuccessful attempts at alliances and take-overs, all aimed at mitigating or eliminating competition, punctuated the tumultuous relationships among the competing groups in the Far East. Standard Oil, with large markets and virtually no crude oil outside the Western Hemisphere, was particularly interested in acquiring companies with crude oil reserves, and even before the First World War made several unsuccessful overtures aimed at obtaining control of British Petroleum, Shell and Royal Dutch. A number of co-operative moves between the last two led, in 1907, to their amalgamation and the creation of Royal Dutch/Shell with the present 60–40 division of interest. Both companies were fully integrated when they merged.

British Petroleum (then Anglo-Persian) got its start in Persia in 1908, financed largely by Burmah Oil, and supported by the British Government.[10] Its two other major sources of oil were in Iraq and Kuwait (the latter a concession jointly owned with Gulf Oil). In Iraq, Anglo-Persian, Royal Dutch/Shell and a German interest had obtained a concession from the Ottoman government before the First World War. After the war the French were granted the German interest and a group of American companies, with the help of the American government, succeeded in obtaining an equal share with the others.[11]

In the meantime the crude oil production of Venezuela, the other major world producer outside the United States, had also come under the control of the same group of companies, except for British Petroleum, as dominated Europe and Asia.[12] BP was excluded because it was deemed to be a government-owned company and the Venezuelan government did not permit companies owned by foreign governments to obtain oil concessions. Royal Dutch/Shell drilled the first commercial well in Venezuela in 1914. Standard Oil of Indiana and Gulf were its most successful rivals and the three companies accounted for nearly all of Venezuela's output at the end of the First World War. Nevertheless, Jersey Standard quickly obtained control of half of the country's production through the acquisition of Standard of Indiana's interest, Creole and, together with Shell, half of Gulf's interest in Mene Grande.[13] At that time Venezuela was the largest producing country in the world outside the United States and the USSR.

Two factors facilitated the virtual monopolization of the major new oil resources of the world. In the Middle East, where governments, often newly established and strongly under the influence of

European powers, were weak and inexperienced, concessions were granted over virtually the whole territory of some countries and for very long periods. From the oil companies' point of view there were good reasons for this, including the enormous risk and expense involved in exploring and developing production in unknown and often extremely inhospitable areas. Nevertheless the result was the effective exclusion of competition from newcomers and the prospect of consolidating the control of the group of companies that obtained (or bought into) the concessions. Second, in both the Middle East and in Latin America concession rights could be bought and sold. This did bring in newcomers: Gulf in Kuwait; Exxon, Mobil and Texaco in Saudi Arabia, for example, but only on terms that ensured no independent competition. In Venezuela, Exxon and Shell were able to buy out their independent interests and consolidate their control along with that of Gulf.

As an exception, France had obtained a share in the Iraq Petroleum Company. This was possible only because of the inter-governmental negotiations over the future of the Middle East following the end of the First World War.[14] The majors were also very much concerned to prevent Italian oil interests from obtaining a foothold in the Middle East and at the time of the formation of the Iranian Consortium went to great lengths to ensure that Ente Nazionale Idrocarburi (ENI), then under the leadership of Enrico Mattei, was excluded.[15]

Thus, before the Second World War the crude oil reserves of the Middle East, Venezuela, and south-east Asia were under the control of seven companies plus the Compagnie Française des Pétroles with its 23.75 per cent interest in the Iraq Petroleum Company. In spite of joint ownerships and operations, numerous alliances and even attempts at establishing outright cartels in some markets, the companies were in competition with each other, especially in product markets. Each rapidly expanded investment in pipelines, refining facilities and distribution networks. Some companies, notably British Petroleum and Gulf, were 'long' on crude, producing more than they used in their own operations and selling so far as possible to other majors on long-term contracts. Each was interested in using its own crude in its own refineries but making joint arrangements to deal with imbalances between crude supplies, refinery needs, distribution facilities and markets. Until the early 1970s, when most of the major crude oil producing countries that had not already done so either nationalized or took equity control over the subsidiaries producing their oil, the dominant position of these seven companies in all stages of the industry, though diminishing, was maintained.[16]

8

Effects of integration

Because of integration each individual company could in principle adjust its output at each stage of the industry to the requirements of later stages. For example, its liftings of crude oil could be adjusted to its refinery needs, these in turn could be estimated with reference to marketing needs. In other words, each such company would in principle attempt to adjust supply to demand within the integrated enterprise. If an entire industry consisted of only a few integrated companies behaving in this manner and if these companies refrained from price competition with each other in the market for end products (which, for a wholly integrated company is the only place where final sales are made) then for the industry as a whole, supply would be adjusted to demand very smoothly at the prevailing level of prices.

In an industry based on the processing of a raw material, a common way of attempting to mitigate price competition in the market for end products is to attempt to ensure that all companies pay roughly the same price for the raw materials. This reduces cost differences among them and thus reduces their incentive to compete on the basis of cost. In the international oil industry this result was to some extent achieved before the Second World War by the use of the so-called 'basing point' pricing system.[17] After the war, with the development of the very large reserves discovered in Kuwait and Saudi Arabia, a different mechanism was established, as we shall see.

In any event, one of the effects of integration, when companies were few and willing to adhere to a few co-operative rules of the game, was to permit the development of the international industry with a relatively smooth adjustment of supply to a rapidly rising demand. The control of the markets for the crude oil of the exporting countries in the developing world, as well as of their crude oil production, gave the industrial countries confidence in the security of their oil supplies – especially Britain, whose government was much concerned with the importance of oil for military purposes.[18] So long as the refining and distribution of oil was controlled by the same companies that controlled crude oil production, the ability of the oil-producing countries to expropriate the companies was severely limited because of their inability to sell and market their oil.[19] In spite of this, however, in times of crisis there were sometimes calls for military action by the industrial countries to protect 'their' oil.

Even if it could be argued that integration, combined with the dominance of the industry by a few companies, had advantages, there is no question that on a global scale it raised problems of policy for both companies and governments since the integration of the companies overlaid a world of national states. The interests of neither host nor home governments were necessarily coincident with those of the companies. Conflicts were inevitable and some eventually became so serious as to bring about a change in the international structure of the industry. The chief sources of conflict between companies and governments related to the companies' unilateral control and management of supply, control of crude oil prices and of government revenues.

Control and management of supply

The development of the very large oil resources that had been discovered in Saudi Arabia and Kuwait before the Second World War had to wait until after the war when the necessary resources could be released. The companies hoped to ensure that the new production could be brought into world markets without disruptive effects either on prices or on existing producers. Without careful management of the rate of supply some higher cost output elsewhere, for example, in Venezuela, would be rapidly displaced, with severe economic and perhaps political consequences for the host country, to say nothing of the effect on the investments of the companies there.

Except in Iran the companies producing the oil of the Middle East were consortia composed of various combinations of the international companies including, in Iraq, the Compagnie Française des Pétroles. Some of these companies, for example, British Petroleum and Gulf had more oil at their disposal than they could use in their own refineries, while others, for example Mobil and CFP, were short of oil. Arrangements had to be made to regulate the total output of each crude oil producing subsidiary and to permit those partners desiring to lift more than their equity proportion of oil to buy from others whose entitlement was greater than their requirements.[20]

The amount of oil produced from any given country was thus determined according to the policies and strategies of the major companies. Moreover, if the companies wanted to reduce output from any country with which they were in conflict, they could easily increase output elsewhere to supply their markets.

The most serious incident of this kind arose in Iran in the early 1950s. Iran was the only major exporting country in the Middle East whose oil was not controlled by a consortium but by a single company – the Anglo-Iranian Oil Company. The Iranian government, in dispute over revenues with the AIOC, nationalized the company. AIOC was able effectively to prevent the government from selling any of the 'nationalized' oil on the ground that the nationalization was illegal and that therefore the oil belonged to the company. The company was able to make up the oil supplies it needed for its operations from its concessions in Iraq and Kuwait. This event was often cited by Middle East politicians and others as an outstanding example of the way in which the international companies denied the oil-exporting countries their rightful 'sovereignty' over their natural resources.[21]

We have already noted that the concession system made it easier for a few companies virtually to monopolize the oil resources of the world outside the United States and the communist countries. The Iraq government once tried to modify the system and acquire greater flexibility in awarding concessions, but failed to do so.[22] In the 1970s the ability of the Libyan government to award smaller concessions to independent companies was one factor helping to undermine the multinational structure of the industry.[23] Some governments saw no alternative to outright nationalization as a means of asserting their sovereign control, for the companies persistently refused, almost to the bitter end in the 1970s, any participation by governments in the ownership of their operating subsidiaries.

Unless a government partner was prepared to sell its oil to the other partners on acceptable terms,[24] equity participation by governments in these subsidiaries would have undermined one of the major advantages of integration – the ability to regulate the off-take of oil in accordance with downstream requirements and to maintain barriers against downstream competition of newcomers with access to low-cost crude. Prices at which oil was sold or transferred to affiliates were very much higher than costs of production.

On the other hand, the oil companies could hardly have expected the governments of the oil-exporting countries to acquiesce indefinitely in foreign control of their major natural resource. Oil is an exhaustible resource; oil production is a mining operation, and the demand for national control over such a resource would certainly have been enforced as soon as governments were strong enough to do so. There was considerable political controversy over this issue even within those countries, such as Saudi Arabia and Kuwait, whose governments, unlike that of Iraq, were on balance content with the operations of the companies, apart from their ever-present desire for increased revenues.

Integration and control of prices

The crude oil supplies owned by the integrated majors were, for the most part, either transferred to their refining affiliates or sold on long-term contracts to other integrated majors who themselves produced less crude oil than they used in their refineries. In consequence, very little crude appeared on the open market and there was therefore no market price for crude oil. Before 1950 the revenues of the oil-exporting countries in the Middle East were based on the amount of oil exported (the so-called 'tonnage royalty'). The exporting countries were not therefore concerned with the 'transfer prices' at which their oil moved from the producing to the refining affiliates of the companies.[25]

On the other hand, these same transfer prices were of considerable importance to the oil-importing countries some of whom at times objected to the cost of imported oil. For example, before the war the delivered price of oil from the Middle East was equated to that from the Gulf of Mexico. During the war the British Auditor General objected to the British navy having to pay prices for bunker fuel at the Persian Gulf that included freight costs from the Gulf of Mexico and he forced a reduction in prices. After the war the United States government complained about the prices charged by Aramco for oil supplied to Europe under the Marshall Plan and took the matter to court.[26]

In the early 1960s the refusal of the companies to accept a protest by the Ceylonese government over the level of prices charged by the companies for products led to the expropriation of the distribution facilities of the companies. Countries whose markets were important to the companies, such as Japan and those of western Europe, were in a better position to force reductions in prices than were weaker countries such as Ceylon and other small developing countries.[27]

The crude oil exporting countries acquired a vital interest in the transfer prices of the companies only after 1950 when the so-called '50/50' division of profits between them and the companies was negotiated. At this point the question of transfer prices and their importance for government revenues moved to the centre of the stage.

Prices, taxes and host government revenues

After the war it had been becoming increasingly clear to the companies that the revenues of their host countries in the Middle East would have to be increased. Understandably, the companies wanted to reduce the cost to themselves of any such increase. Aramco, the consortium producing Saudi oil, was an American company registered in the United States, and as such was subject to United States income taxes. If it paid revenues to its foreign host government in the form of taxes on income, such taxes could be offset against the United States tax liability on foreign income. The saving on United States taxes might more than offset the increased payments to Saudi Arabia, particularly since income attributed to crude oil production received special tax concessions under the United States tax laws.[28]

In the absence of a market price for crude oil it was necessary to find a way of valuing the crude in order to calculate an income for income tax purposes. In 1950 the Aramco partners decided to publish, or 'post', a price for crude oil at which it would in principle be sold or transferred to their refineries. The difference between this price, less any discounts permitted by governments, and an agreed cost of production would be the income to be taxed at a rate of 50 per cent by the government. Royalties, which in the United States are normally 'expensed', or treated as costs, were included in the government's share of the profits — a sore point with the host governments and one quickly corrected when OPEC came on the scene. This system was extended in the early 1950s to other oil-producing countries in the Middle East and thus gave them a vested interest in the level of posted prices since their revenues depended on them as much as on the volume of oil sold.

The emergence of OPEC and the erosion of integration

Towards the end of the 1950s competition in product markets began to force down the prices of products, especially in Europe, which meant that the revenues of the integrated companies were reduced while the tax price of oil was maintained. The companies cut posted prices in 1959 and 1960, arguing that the reduction was necessary to bring the prices of oil in line with the lower product prices. The consequent reduction in tax revenues was unacceptable to the governments of the producing countries who responded with the formation of the Organization of Petroleum Exporting Countries (OPEC). OPEC did not succeed in restoring the level of posted prices but from that time on the structure and operation of the international oil industry began gradually to change.

During the 1960s some financial concessions were obtained from the companies as OPEC organized itself and formulated its demands. Although the companies were fully aware of the 'radical' movements in the Middle East and north Africa, they apparently did not realize fully the extent to which the post-war spirit of nationalism and resentment of 'neo-imperialism' had spread even to the conservative countries of the Middle East, such as Saudi Arabia and Kuwait, whose governments were friendly to the companies and to the 'West' but who could not ignore the sentiments of their own people and of those in the Arab world generally. Consequently the companies did not fully understand how far the OPEC countries were prepared to go to achieve their objectives.[29]

In 1968 OPEC issued a 'Declaratory statement of petroleum policy' in which its objectives were clearly stated. These included the demand that governments should participate in the equity of the oil-producing companies and be able to operate directly in exploration and production, and that they should control posted prices. These objectives were achieved to some extent between 1970 and 1973. They were achieved fully in the aftermath of the Arab–Israeli war of that year.[30]

The assumption of ownership and/or control of their crude oil operations by the governments of the oil-producing countries broke a major link in the integration that had characterized the operations of the international companies. This in itself, however, was not a shock to the international oil economy for the companies in fact continued to lift most of the oil produced by their old operating companies; the 'oil shock' of the 1970s resulted from the way in which the OPEC governments used their control over prices.

The international oil industry is still a multinational industry as defined at the beginning of this paper, but to a diminishing extent. The oil-exporting countries were able in the first instance to take over the control of the downstream physical operations of the international companies without significant disruption of the physical flows of oil (except, of course, for those accompanying the war itself). The 'operational' integration of the system was not seriously disrupted. At the present time, however, more or less 'arm's length' trade in crude oil has steadily replaced the previous interaffiliate trade of the companies. Integration of production and refining is taking place in some of the national companies in the Middle East as they develop their exports of refined products. In at least one country, Kuwait, refinery and distribution systems are apparently being acquired to handle its products. It is too soon to try to envisage the future structure of the international industry, but if, as is predicted by many, oil becomes 'just another commodity', the multinational structure of the industry as I have defined it will have disappeared.

Notes

1 See *BP Statistical Review of World Energy* (Annual Editions).
2 Mira Wilkins has a good discussion of the US oil companies in her *The Emergence of Multinational Enterprise: American Business Abroad from the Colonial Era to 1914* (Cambridge, Mass: Harvard University Press, 1970). See also Ralph W. and Muriel Hidy, *Pioneering in Big Business, 1882–1911, History of Standard Oil Company (New Jersey)* (New York: Harper and Bros, 1955); and George S. Gibb and Evelyn H. Knowlton, *The Resurgent Years, 1911–1927, History of Standard Oil Company (New Jersey)* (New York, Harper and Bros, 1956).
3 For the details of the early history of British Petroleum see R. W. Ferrier, *The History of The British Petroleum Company. Vol. I. The Developing Years 1901–1932* (Cambridge University Press, 1982). For Royal Dutch/Shell see F. C. Garretson, *History of the Royal Dutch* (Leiden, Brill, 4 vols, 1953–57). A brief history of each of the international major companies can be found in Edith T. Penrose, *The Large International Firm in Developing Countries: The International Petroleum Industry* (London, Allen and Unwin, 1968), Chapter IV.
4 Each of the international oil 'companies' consists of a group of separately incorporated subsidiary or affiliate companies linked together by an intricate chain of shareholdings. There is usually a head office and an over-arching holding company. I use the terms 'company' or 'group' interchangeably to refer to the entire collection of companies known under the usual names, e.g. Exxon, British Petroleum or Royal Dutch/Shell, unless qualified, e.g. 'operating company', 'refining company', or Iraq Petroleum Company. See E. T. Penrose, op. cit., and United States Federal Trade Commission, *The International Petroleum Cartel*, US Senate Select Committee on Small Business, Staff Report to the Federal Trade Commission, 82nd Congress Committee Print No. 6, 22 August 1952.
5 A good discussion of the stages of the industry can be found in M. A. Adelman, *The World Petroleum Market* (Baltimore, Md.: Johns Hopkins University Press for Resources for the Future, 1972).
6 See Gibb and Knowlton, op. cit.
7 See the documents published by the US House of Representatives, *Current Antitrust Problems*, Hearings Before Antitrust Subcommittee (No. 5) of the Committee on the Judiciary, 84th Congress, 1st session, Part 1, Serial No. 3.
8 Penrose, op. cit., pp. 122–4.
9 Robert Henriques, *Marcus Samuel. First Viscount Bearstead and Founder of the Shell Transport and Trading Company* (London, 1960).
10 Ferrier, op. cit.
11 Marian Kent, *Oil and Empire: British Policy and Mesopotamian Oil, 1900–1929* (London, Macmillan, 1976), Chapter 7.
12 Federal Trade Commission, op. cit.
13 John Blair, *The Control of Oil* (New York, Pantheon Books, 1976), Part I.

14 Kent, op. cit.
15 Dow Votaw, *The Six-Legged Dog: Mattei and ENI – A Study in Power*, Institute of Business and Economic Research, University of California (Berkeley, University of California Press, 1964).
16 There were, of course, nationalizations before 1970, notably in Mexico, Iran, Iraq, and Algeria.
17 The Federal Trade Commission Report, op. cit., contains a good discussion of the basing point system.
18 See Ferrier, op. cit.
19 A problem that arose for both Iran and Mexico when they nationalized their oil.
20 For a discussion of these arrangements see Penrose, op. cit., Chapter V.
21 The conflict between the AIOC and the Iranian government was hopelessly entangled in Iranian politics and dragged on from 1947 until the fall of the government of Musaddiq in 1953. The nationalization was not in principle reversed but a consortium was established to produce Iranian oil consisting of the seven majors plus CFP and Iricon. The latter was composed of five American independent oil companies and had a 5 per cent shareholding in the Iranian consortium.
22 In the early days of its concession Iraq tried to institute a 'plot' system which would have given it some flexibility in offering concessions to newcomers. See Edith and E. F. Penrose, *Iraq: International Relations and National Development* (London and Boulder, Colo., Ernest Benn and Westview Press, 1978), Chapter 6.
23 Frank C. Waddams, *The Libyan Oil Industry* (London, Croom Helm, 1980), Chapters 12, 13.
24 As did C. S. Gulbenkian, who had a 5 per cent ownership in the IPC.
25 See Zuhayr Mikdashi, *A Financial Analysis of Middle Eastern Oil Concessions: 1901–65* (New York, Praeger, 1966).
26 John Blair, op. cit.
27 See Penrose, op. cit.: 229–30.
28 ibid.
29 Suspicion of foreign control of oil resources was not confined to the developing countries. Even in the United States federal law restricts foreign participation in US enterprises associated with the development of mineral resources owned by the Federal Government. Canada's recent attempts to restrict US ownership of its oil resources created a great deal of controversy for a while but has now been abandoned.
30 Ian Seymour, *OPEC Instrument of Change* (London, Macmillan, 1980).

Chapter two

National oil companies with reference to the Middle East 1900–73

Dr N. Ghorban, Mid-Continental Bank and Trust (WI), London

Emergence of the national oil companies

National oil companies have emerged in many countries of the world regardless of the status of their economic development, their geographical position or the political philosophy of their respective governments. The activities of these national oil companies range from full scale monopolies running an integrated operation of those State oil companies holding some interest in oil refining on behalf of the government. The desire of governments in the past fifty years to enter the oil business is based on a variety of reasons which have changed as the structure of the world petroleum industry moved through different stages of its development. The main arguments often presented in defence of the establishment of State oil venture were as follows:[1]

1. The international oil companies may fail to develop the oil resources of the country fully because they have other interests elsewhere.
2. A State-owned oil company adds to national security, especially if there are indigenous sources of oil and gas within the country.
3. The energy requirement and its development is considered to be among government responsibilities.
4. The national oil company can enter into a variety of barter agreements and state-to-state deals, especially with the Eastern Bloc countries, something that international oil companies do not provide.
5. There is considerable hostility towards the international oil companies and for political reasons some governments do not want to be seen as leaving oil matters entirely to the discretion of these firms.

In the case of developed countries that had little or no internal oil and gas resources, the national oil company was developed to add to the security of oil supplies which were dependent on the multi-national oil companies and to search for new sources of oil. In Italy, Ente Nazionale Idrocarburi (ENI), the State-owned company, was formed in 1953 but was based largely on Azienda Generale Italiana Petroli (AGIP) itself dating from 1924. The objective of ENI, as laid down in the 1953 law setting it up, was to promote and undertake new activities in hydrocarbon and steam operation, to explore for and to exploit hydrocarbon deposits in the Po Valley (Italy) and to engage in production, manufacture and commerce in hydrocarbons.

In France, L'Entreprise de Recherches et d'Activités Petroliers, a wholly State-owned company, was formed by a government decree in 1965 which merged two other companies to form ERAP as from January 1966. ERAP's main objectives were to provide France with a cheap and independent supply of oil and to compete with the majors.[2] In Latin America, Argentina established its State oil company in 1910; But in 1927, the State established Yacimientos Petroliferos Fiscales (YPF) which was given monopoly right to all oil exploration and production. Petroleo Brasileiro (Petrobras), the Brazilian State company, was incorporated in 1954 and was given a mandate to engage in all aspects of the oil industry. National oil companies were also established in other developing importing countries, mainly to help governments to reduce or contain the activities of the large international oil companies in their oil industries.[3]

In the oil exporting countries, national oil companies (NOCs) were created for a variety of economic or political reasons. The governments used these companies as an administrative network to deal with the oil industry. Furthermore, the establishment of the State oil company satisfied national pride and gave a sense of achievement. In some cases the establishment of the NOC was in conjunction with nationalization of the foreign oil companies. In the case of Mexico, Petroleas Mexicanas (Pemex) was given the mandate to take over the administration of Mexico's oil industry after the Nationalization Act of 1948.

World petroleum markets during the establishments of NOCs

The emergence of the national oil companies of Mexico in 1938 and Iran in 1951, preceded the nationalization of the oil industry in these countries. In both cases, the multinational oil companies put embargos on the oil produced and successfully managed to curtail the activities of the newly born State oil company to that of domestic distribution of petroleum products in their respective countries.

The structure of the world petroleum industry at the time of the formation of these companies and for many years after (up until the 1970s) was dominated by the seven international oil companies; Standard Oil Company (now Exxon), Socony Vacuum Oil Company (now Mobil), Gulf Oil Company (now bought by Chevron), Standard Oil Company of California (Socal), Texas Oil Company (Texaco), Anglo-Iranian Oil Company (now BP) and Royal Dutch-Shell Group. These companies directly or indirectly controlled most of the world's petroleum business by owning reserves and production as well as transportation and marketing facilities through their integrated networks. Table 2.1 shows the extent of the control of the major international oil companies on the world petroleum business.[4]

Table 2.1 Major oil companies and world petroleum

Estimated oil reserves held by seven international petroleum companies January 1949, excluding the USA, in billion barrels, in the Eastern Bloc		*Crude oil production of seven international petroleum companies in 1949 in thousand barrels per day, excluding USA and per day, excluding refining capacity of US, USSR, Hungary, Rumania*	*Crude oil refining capacity controlled by seven international petroleum companies in 1950 in thousand barrels*
Total for seven companies	41.3	3,074.3	3,107.2
Total estimated	50.3	4,491.3	4,010.9
Total seven companies %	82.1	88.1	77.5

The control of the seven major oil companies over transportation facilities in 1950 was approximately two-thirds of the privately owned tanker fleet and they owned most of the pipelines outside the United States. After the Second World War and through the 1950s, the rate of increase in production capacity around the world was higher than the rate of increase in demand for petroleum products in spite of the reconstruction efforts of the post-war era. When the Iranian government nationalized Anglo-Iranian Oil Company (AIOC), nearly one-third of Middle East production was lost. The ease with which the loss of Iranian production was replaced by other countries of the Middle East is an indication of the extent of production capacity developed between 1948 and 1952.

Towards the end of the 1950s, increased competition by the independent oil companies changed the terms under which concessions were obtained in the Middle East. In addition to that increase, competition in crude oil and product markets led to reduction of posted prices. The reaction from the producers was manifested in the formation of the Organization of Petroleum Exporting Countries (OPEC). During the 1960s, when many of the national oil companies of the Middle East were formed, the surplus of production capacity over demand persisted. However, major international oil companies and the independent oil companies were involved in exploration and production of oil both within OPEC countries and outside. This meant that national oil companies had difficulty selling oil in the open market without giving substantial discounts.[5]

Direct sales of crude by the national oil companies

The major international oil companies which were producing crude oil through jointly-owned subsidiaries in the world avoided arms-length transactions in the markets as much as possible. During the period under consideration, crude oil was sold mainly to other affiliates of the same or similar integrated company for processing. The majors had a competitive advantage over those which did not have access to equity oil and open competition in sales of crude oil in the markets would have only helped their competitors who had a higher average cost of supply. But, regardless of the attempt to limit sales of crude oil in the open markets, more oil was entering the markets in the 1960s mainly through other independent companies and government sales.[6]

The national oil companies had very little crude oil available to them for export apart from their entitlement to royalties which was payable, if desired by the producers in kind. None of the producers used this option in this respect mainly because there was a significant difference between realized prices that they could obtain in the crude oil market, and the posted prices that were the basis of the company payments. However, this situation was changed as the oil from new joint venture and contract agreements became available to these companies.[7]

In 1966, the representatives of national oil companies in OPEC gathered in Caracas for the first time to discuss general policies. One of the issues discussed in this meeting was concern over future activities of the national oil companies in direct sale of crude oil in the markets. It was agreed that the entry of those companies into the market should be conducted in a way not to destabilize oil prices and there should be co-operation among the national oil companies to minimize the effect of their entry into the markets. Up until 1973 sales of crude oil by the national oil companies in the Middle East were very limited. In Kuwait, KNPC had no significant sales of crude oil on its own account. Petromin's sales of crude oil from the participation agreement did not start until 1973. NIOC's share of oil from the joint venture agreements was usually marketed by the foreign parties, but the company was involved in sales of crude on a basis of barter deals with Eastern Europe. During the period under consideration, the national oil companies were not price cutters in the markets and they followed the pricing policy of OPEC.

The autonomy and motivation of the national oil companies

International oil firms with a large number of shareholders are self-governing organizations, whose managements are in principle responsible to the shareholders. The administrators of the national oil companies are not autonomous in the sense that they have to carry out the oil policy of their governments. The government as the only shareholder of these companies can effectively control their operations. All the national oil companies during the period under consideration were basically highly centralized. They had an assembly of representatives from various government organizations similar to a Board of Directors of a private firm. NIOC's Board of Directors did not include outsiders but government control was exercised through a body called 'The Shareholders Representatives' which consisted of seven ministers headed by the Prime Minister.

The Board of Directors of KNPC had ten members of whom six represented the government and four represented the private shareholders. In Saudi Arabia, Petromin's Board included the government representatives and was headed by the Minister of Oil. But all this does not imply that the managers of the national oil companies based their decisions on direct instructions from the government. There were a number of experienced and well-informed technocrats within each of these national oil companies whose views were respected by the government officials and, when it came to implementation of general policies, the managers of the national oil companies had an almost free hand. Most of the decisions at this stage were taken at the company level, which includes construction, expansion of local facilities and other relevant matters. In this respect the national oil companies can be considered as large, autonomous, bureaucracies inside their country.

The national oil companies of the Middle East have another interesting feature in common which is the political weight that the top management has within the country's ruling group. The influence and importance of the national oil company somehow depends on the relationships between the general manager and the person or persons who hold political power in the country. General managers of the NIOC up until the revolution in 1978 were veteran politicians and former Prime Ministers. These people had direct access to the highest authority in Iran, the Shah, and on a number of occasions resisted carrying out government plans and proposed their own. The involvement of nearly all the chairmen of NIOC in politics before reaching their positions in the company contributed to the unique web of favouritism which normally exist in government organizations in the Middle East.

In Saudi Arabia, also, the role of Petromin is partly dependent on the personality and political weight of its Governor. Political favouritism and nepotism were probably as strong as in Iran, although they are more obscure to the foreigners. As the Board of Directors of Petromin consisted of a number of ministers and high ranking authorities from different government organizations, the process of decision making was different to that of NIOC, which had to get the approval from the government ministers committee who were not members of the Board.

Integration by the national oil companies

Nearly all the national oil companies in the Middle East were planning to become fully integrated oil companies during the period of this study. Article 2(f) of the Statutes of the General Petroleum and Mineral Organization, Article 4(a) of the Statutes of the National Iranian Oil Company and Article 5(1) of the 'Articles of Association' of the Kuwait National Petroleum Company all indicated the desire of the government to see the full integration of the State oil company. The national oil companies were commissioned to engage in exploration, production, transportation, refining of crude oil and marketing of petroleum products either inside or outside the country.[8]

During the 1960s the planners of national oil companies in the Middle East believed that vertical integration is a necessary condition for the efficient operation of an oil firm although the classic argument in favour of integration does not really apply to the national oil companies. The major international oil companies, considering the imperfections of the market and the degree of monopoly, integrated whenever they saw the possibility of more profits. The decision to integrate downstream (refining and marketing) or upstream (crude oil production) was not based on any particular profitable model or general policy of these firms.

Advantages attributed to vertical integration of an oil firm were:

(a) assured sources of crude oil and outlets for the company's products;
(b) advantages associated with large scale operations; and
(c) tax benefits.

None of the above arguments can be extended to the operations of the national oil companies. Some were in charge of production, refining, transportation and sale of products in their respective country. The State oil companies had no tax advantages as a result of integration and their respective governments ultimately controlled the source of crude oil. National oil companies realized that the desire to control oil from the well-head to the petrol station, which was considered to be an important factor in the success of multinational oil companies, was neither the most easily attained nor the most profitable from the point of view of producing countries. Many of the long-term objectives of the national oil companies could be achieved with limited involvement in the downstream activities outside their countries. Downstream investment in refining and distribution may not add to the disposition of crude oil or greater return on the investment of these companies.[9]

Political nature of the national oil companies

The events which led to the formation of the national oil companies and their subsequent evolution indicate that internal and external political forces played a major role in the history of these companies. National oil companies of the Middle East cannot be judged wholly on economic criteria. They are sometimes assigned by their respective governments to fulfil political and social tasks in which a private oil company would not wish to participate. It must be said that all successful oil companies are well aware of the political nature of the oil business. The difference between a national oil company and international oil companies in this respect is that the involvement of the former in the oil business is primarily based on serving the interest of one country, while the latter's activities are motivated by their profitable growth on a global basis. Any evolution of the activities of the national oil companies must give due consideration to the political nature of the problem rather than be based on the model of the international oil companies.

The establishment and development of the National Iranian Oil Company is an example of how the external and internal political forces affected the operation of these companies. NIOC was formed following the nationalization of the oil industry in Iran, which was a political decision without adequate study of its possible economic results. The negotiations for the settlement of the dispute between Anglo-Iranian Oil Company and Iran failed mainly due to the argument on the issues of compensation which was politically not acceptable to Dr Musaddiq. As a result of this the National Oil Company lost a golden opportunity to begin its activities with full control over the production, refining and export of Iranian crude oil and products.

The Consortium agreement was reached as a result of a political settlement between Iran, the United Kingdom and the United States. The development of the Iraq National Oil Company is another example of the role of politics in the affairs of the State oil venture. INOC was formed in 1964 but its development and role in the oil industry in Iraq was dependent on the outcome of the negotiations between the IPC group and the Iraqi government on the issue of expropriation of their assets. Initially, the government and the national oil company formulated a deal with the owners of IPC which would have enhanced the role of INOC in the petroleum industry of Iraq but the agreement came under heavy political attack by sections of the ruling party which claimed that its implementation would be a victory for the oil companies and 'imperialism'. The agreement was not ratified and the development of the State oil company entered a different phase.

In the case of Kuwait National Petroleum Company and Petromin there were no similar internal and external political forces involved in the early years of the development of their national oil companies. However, the power and authority of these companies and other national oil companies in the Middle East were often altered according to what governments wanted of their role in the country's oil industry.

A comparative recapitulation

The national oil companies of oil producing countries were not established for economic reasons or out of market necessity following fundamental changes in the petroleum industry. They were mostly developed as a reaction of their government to the operations of multinational oil companies or as a result of nationalization acts. Once formed, they were given responsibility for domestic operations. Most of the national oil companies in the Middle East began their operations by taking over the distribution of the petroleum products within their countries. The governments usually gave them monopolistic rights to market products inside the country. The State oil companies have built up their own installations and in some cases taken over the existing outlets owned by foreign companies for distribution of petroleum products in the local market.

There are similarities in the objectives of the national oil companies of the oil exporting countries particularly in the Middle East. They were usually given the mandate to undertake all petroleum operations within the country. But as the development and exploitation of a nation's oil and gas resources is a very big task, the petroleum laws allow the assistance of large international firms in one way or another. The areas relinquished by the foreign companies were also allocated for exploration activities of the State oil company. In Iran, NIOC signed its first contract agreement in 1966. According to this type of agreement foreign oil companies became partners or contractors for NIOC. In 1968 the Kuwait government granted KNPC a petroleum concession to jointly operate with a foreign oil company. In Saudi Arabia there are joint venture agreements between Petromin and French oil companies. In Iraq similar agreements were signed between INOC and ERAP, the French State oil company, in 1967. Another common objective of the national oil companies is integration and diversification. The statutes of most of these companies provide for their engagement individually or in participation with others in both downstream and upstream operations inside or outside their respective countries. While some of the national oil companies have achieved full integration in the oil industry of their country, their efforts to expand and diversify activities beyond their borders have so far been limited. The third common objective of the national oil companies was supervision of concession agreements and their implementation, but, in effect, governments generally carried out this function and national oil companies' roles were limited to technical and operational supervision rather than control over finance, pricing and level of oil output.

Beside similarities of objectives, national oil companies all depend on their governments for financing of projects. The revenues of domestic marketing of petroleum products are often not adequate for budget autonomy and the companies have to keep prices of products at levels demanded by their governments regardless of increases in their operating costs. Major expansion plans of the national oil companies are also controlled by their governments and are adjusted to the overall development plans within their countries. Some of the national oil companies have sold crude oil or petroleum products to various customers in the period considered here, but they had no pricing policy of their own. The government gave specific pricing instructions for such sales. KNPC was not allowed to sell substantial quantities of crude oil which was the responsibility of the oil ministry. NIOC and Petromin were involved in sales of substantial quantities of oil following the government's pricing policy.

As the oil industry expanded rapidly in the Middle East, the task of the national oil companies was narrowed down by the establishment of other State owned entities. In Iran the National Iranian Gas Company and National Petrochemical Company, which were subsidiaries of the NIOC eventually became independent. In Saudi Arabia, Petromin's role which included responsibility for all the oil and mineral resources, was reduced to refining, transportation, distribution and marketing of oil internally and abroad. In Kuwait also, the responsibilities for oil production, refining for export and petrochemicals were given to different State-owned companies. In general the activities of the national oil companies, which in most cases involved gas projects, petrochemical ventures and other activities, were narrowed down mainly to oil.

It must be noted that most of the national oil companies played an important role in advising their governments on oil and gas policies. During the period considered, these companies employed a large number of engineers, economists and oil technicians who were in good positions to advise the government on its projects. So, indirectly, they influenced the overall decisions of governments *vis-à-vis* pricing, joint venture agreements and other major oil and gas projects.

The differences among the national oil companies in the Middle East are mainly their size and the role which they play in the oil industry of their respective countries. NIOC employed nearly 40,000 people by 1973 as against KNPC's 1,800 which consists of more than 80 per cent non-Kuwaitis. Petromin and INOC's workforce were also small compared to NIOC. By 1973, NIOC was active in all aspects of the oil industry in Iran. In the southern oil fields nearly all of the operations were controlled by the national oil company. Exploration for oil was generally left to foreign oil companies who would act as NIOC's contractors. The company was involved in some exploration and development activities on its own, or in partnership with other oil companies. NIOC was also responsible for the sale of crude oil and petroleum products on its own account.

KNPC on the other hand was mainly responsible for the domestic marketing and sales of petroleum products since its establishment in 1960. A major difference between KNPC and all the other national oil companies in the Middle East was that it was 40 per cent owned by the private shareholders. Petromin controlled three companies which were involved in exploration and drilling activities but, unlike NIOC, it did not have any significant role in actual oil production within the Kingdom. Crude oil production was carried out by the Arabian American Company (ARAMCO) which was owned by four of the major American international oil companies.

The national oil companies in the Middle East rapidly grew into large semi-autonomous bureaucracies inside their countries. Governments were usually the final decision makers with regard to the development of these companies and they took those decisions, not on the basis of profitable growth of the company, but with regard to their own overall political and economic objectives. The national oil companies also influenced government decisions on the country's oil and gas policies by being organizations which contained some of the best experts on the country's oil and gas industry.

Notes

1 L. E. Grayson, *National Oil Companies* (Norwich, 1981), Chapter 1.
2 ibid., Chapter 4 for ENI and Chapter 5 for ERAP.
3 E. Penrose, *The Large International Firm in Developing Countries. The International Petroleum Industry* (London, 1968).
4 Federal Trade Commission Report, *The International Petroleum Cartel* (Washington, 1952): 23– 5.
5 M. A. Adelman, *The World Petroleum Market* (London, 1972), Chapter VI.
6 ibid.: 199.
7 *Petroleum Press Services* May 1967: 163.
8 See (a) General Petroleum and Mineral Organization, published by Petromin (no date or place of publication given): 24. (b) Statutes of the National Iranian Oil Company, 1974, published by NIOC Tehran, Article 4(a): 18. (c) *The Expanding Role of KNPC* (Kuwait National Petroleum Company, Kuwait): 33– 7.
9 Dr Abdulhady Taher, *The Future Role of the National Oil Companies in the World Petroleum Industry*, OPEC Seminar, 10– 12 October 1977 Vienna, Information Department, OPEC: 191.

Chapter three

Oil in developing countries in South America

Mircea Buescu, Catholic University, Rio de Janeiro

This chapter looks at the question of oil in the developing countries of South America. Brazil has been given special attention because of its size, among other reasons. It deals with the period from the Great Depression of 1929, which gave birth to autarchical, interventionist and nationalistic policies in many states, until the early 1970s, the time of the oil crisis. While this paper deals mainly with the Brazilian oil industry, there is not much to report before the 1930s, although oil had been discovered in 1864 and prospecting and production attempts had been made even before the First World War.

Studies of the oil industry usually deal with competition between monopolies. In the case of under-developed countries, they focus on the submission to foreign interests of these countries, and their ensuing efforts to escape this domination. The last years of the Nineteenth century saw the entry of South America into the oil industry. Before then, attempts at exploitation were economically negligible. Oil production started before the First World War in Peru (1896), Argentina (1907), Bolivia (1908), Venezuela (1909), as well as in the Latin American countries of Central America, Trinidad (1897) and Mexico (1901). The existing world-wide economic framework shaped the industry being raised within it through the international division of labour and the part played by the suppliers of raw materials, in this case, the oil companies who utilized their superior technology and capital, lacking in the under-developed world, to re-sell their products to those same countries.

It is claimed that foreign oil companies did not want to invest in Brazil, either to maintain the supply at a low level, or to keep the oil deposits in Brazil as a future reserve. This does not seem convincing. It is much more probable that the economics of production in Brazil were not good enough to justify investment. The first hypothesis does not match with the continuing research of oil reserves by the industry (see Peach-Constantin). It has also been asserted that big companies took no interest in reserves situated too far from the market places, which was detrimental to the more remote countries (see Mosconi). While it is true that the investors' activities were dependent on costs of production and profits, this argument is not justifiable. Argentina is more distant than Brazil and yet was the centre of vigorous activity on the part of the larger companies.

Oil produced was obviously not destined for the producing country, which had no refining facilities and formed a negligible market for products.[1] Meanwhile, international trade provided a source of income for the producing country, which was unable to generate profit alone, lacking both the capital and technology necessary for oil production. While it is true that foreign companies kept the lion's share of profits for themselves, provoking a reaction against them in the future, the long-term advantages to the economy brought about by free trade must not be overlooked.

The two biggest international companies in South America were Standard Oil of New Jersey followed by Royal Dutch-Shell. Industries created in Peru, Bolivia and Ecuador were not very successful, but they did reasonably well in Argentina and exceeded all expectations in Venezuela. In 1930, Latin America produced 16.8 per cent of the world's crude oil, three quarters of which was shared between Venezuela and Mexico. In the 1930s, Venezuela became the world's third largest producer. This period was characterized by efforts on the part of the oil-producing countries of the Third World to expel multinational interests, by way of nationalization. Two main factors influenced this change. First, the national consumption of oil increased with the growth of the economy in these countries and oil products became a determining factor not only for higher living standards but essential to sustain economic development. Second, oil had become indispensable in maintaining defence and national security in a world in which worsening political relations were leading to the outbreak of the Second World War.

A growing dependence on oil was created world-wide because of economic progress and the development of a technology based on oil products. In 1930, liquid fuels represented 14.5 per cent of world-wide energy consumption, 38.3 per cent by 1969, in the same year it had reached 64.6 per cent in Latin America (two-thirds of which were fuel oils). During the 1960s, the consumption of oil products in Latin America increased by 5.8 per cent, nearly twice the rate of population increase. The main reason was the increase in the road haulage industry. By 1969, it consumed 46 per cent of oil products. In 1972, 73.3 per cent of goods were transported by road in Brazil.

International trade and the free-market economy suffered from a loss of confidence at this time giving rise to more nationalist economic policies, growing State intervention and autarchy. Taking control of international companies was essential to protect the countries' defence and national security, the organization of oil production and its products were indispensable for their autonomy. This task became the responsibility of the government. Mosconi, the leading Argentinian proponent of this policy, succinctly explained: 'I believe that the management of our oil reserves can only succeed if based on nationalization of our resources. Successful administration by the Government is possible when correct policy is chosen and implemented for this purpose.' The object of the government would be 'the elimination of all political influence in the industrial and commercial management of the oil industry' – obviously a reference to external political influence.

Governmental intervention started before 1929 in Venezuela (1918), Colombia (1919–27) and Argentina (1922). More decisive measures were taken by Argentina in 1929 when the State company YPF (Yacimentos Petroliferos Fiscales) took complete control of the domestic fuel market. Further north, Mexico started an interventionist policy from 1933, which led to the nationalization of the oil industry in 1939. These changes took different forms throughout the continent. In Venezuela, foreign investment was not suppressed. A limit of 50 per cent was established and then lowered to 40 per cent in 1943, when new restrictions were imposed. In Argentina, the participation of the State in the economy ran parallel with private investment, including foreign companies, within the limits set by the Acts of 1935, 1958, and 1967. Similar mixed policies were established in Colombia (1948, 1950), Ecuador, Bolivia (1942), Chile, Paraguay, and Uruguay (1936 – applying only to the refining industry).[2] Nationalization reinforced these tendencies later.[3] Whatever regime existed, increasing consumption was accompanied by substantial increases in crude oil production and its products.[4]

In 1958, largely thanks to Venezuela, South America as a whole produced a surplus of energy. Oil represented 61 per cent of the total energy production. The oil consumption of two countries, Argentina and Bolivia, was matched by their production. Colombia, Ecuador, Peru and especially, Venezuela, produced an exportable surplus. The other South American countries relied on crude oil imports, and in some cases where refining facilities were lacking, had to import products as well. The provision of refineries had generally followed the pattern of oil discovery. However, this was not the case in Brazil. (See Table 3.1 for comparison of countries, production/consumption figures.)

The ability of some countries to export surplus crude oil,[5] the need of others to import crude for refining, or where facilities were lacking the purchase of refined products,[6] all lent great importance to international trade.

Table 3.1. South America: balance of trade in oil, 1951

	(Millions of barrels/year)	
	Production	Consumption
Argentina	71.0	68.6
Bolivia	1.5	(insignificant)
Brazil	2.2	40.1
Chile	2.0	9.1
Colombia	106.2	8.7
Ecuador	7.4	(insignificant)
Paraguay	—	(insignificant)
Peru	44.0	10.8
Uruguay	—	8.4
Venezuela	1,702.0	32.4

In general, Brazil differed from other Latin American countries in that it was not part of the pioneering group of oil producing countries, where large companies had found and developed oil-fields (Mexico, Venezuela and Argentina). Brazil too undertook a campaign to achieve a 'national' oil industry but in a different economic and political context. For reasons which remain unclear, oil trusts did not seem interested in Brazil, as already mentioned. While ignoring the possibilities for extraction, they meanwhile began marketing oil products and later developed refineries, but they had missed the moment. The tide of nationalization was already prevailing throughout the oil industry, for at that moment, publications were appearing voicing a passionate resistance to foreign encroachment and international monopolies.[7] The campaign for nationalization was launched under the now famous slogan: 'It is our Oil'.

Large-scale efficient exploitation of oil reserves was impossible in Brazil, which lacked the capital, technology and skilled work-force needed. However opposition to the oil trusts, and the desire to create a national industry (no doubt largely influenced by the example of Argentina) matched the nationalistic and autarchical mood of the time. This trend was reinforced by a realization of the importance of oil, not only to develop an independent economy but to guarantee national security. This feeling is understandable in the context of a world on the brink of another world war and economic and political decision making reflected these considerations, even after the war. For example, a speech by President Getulio Vargas claimed in 1950: 'What is essential to our national security, what forms the basis of our national Sovereignty, cannot be left in the hands of foreign interests; it must be done by Brazilians, with a large amount of state intervention to avoid the threat of monopolies.'

The demand for oil products increased dramatically. Economic development and, as elsewhere, an increase in domestic and industrial use, all served to boost oil consumption.[8] Both the birth of the Brazilian car industry in 1955, which became the key industry in Brazil, and the expansion in road transport[9] greatly increased the outlets available to the oil industry. It must be remembered that for Brazil, the oil boom took place within a different economic climate than had existed in neighbouring Latin American countries. It is difficult (although this is open to dispute) to speak of a real take-off in the Brazilian oil industry prior to this having taken place in the immediate post-war period,[10] that is to say, the time when the whole oil question had become of paramount concern. The take-off in oil supposed not just a government dedicated to the progress of its economy, for the existence of a suitable infrastructure, the creation of capital and of a skilled workforce were all necessary for an independent policy to succeed. This independence was qualified, however, since policies were to need the support of international commerce in the post-war economy, when goods and capital began to move normally.

In accordance with the ideology prevailing in Brazil at the time, there was overwhelming support for the idea that only government action would be able to resolve the problems posed by oil: the ability to stand up to monopolies and the need to mobilize the necessary capital, technology and professional workforce. Before this strong government intervention, private-sector attempts at oil exploration and exploitation had had little success. Some progress had been made in developing a trading sector prior to the First World War with the help of foreign investment. After the Depression a refining industry was established with some success. With State intervention, beginning in 1931, efforts to direct and control developments were made, focusing mainly on oil exploration. With this object specialist State bodies were set up, such as the Mineral Production Board (1933). This trend towards State control continued with the 1934 Constitution and the Mines Act of the same year, and was strengthened by the 1937 Constitution which reserved for Brazilians the right to extract oil. More measures followed based on the policy of a nationally-run oil industry.

Decree 395 in 1938 created the National Oil Board – the main organ of government policy. This Board represented a decisive step in furthering government aims, having not only a regulatory role but possessing executive powers relating to oil production and refining.[11] In 1941, the State took control of all oil reserves. Authorization for development was granted through the National Oil Board.

A second major step was taken with the creation of the public limited oil company, Petrobas (Act 2004/1953 and Decree 35508/1954). A State monopoly had been clearly established. From small beginnings in exploration projects, Petrobas soon included refining; today the target is marketing. Crude oil imports were brought under monopoly control in 1963 and in 1964 it was the turn of the refineries. These moves encapsulated the political aim of self-sufficiency in oil. Brazil adopted these policies at a time when the economy was booming. A growing demand for fuel posed a problem in the short-term of finding sufficient quantities at the lowest possible cost. To bridge the gap, efforts were concentrated on constructing refineries, which processed imported crude oil.[12] During this time crude oil imports rose to supply the Brazilian refineries.

Obviously, events in Brazil could not have happened in countries which had begun by selling their oil on the world market. In these countries (Mexico, Argentina, Ecuador and Bolivia), refining facilities had taken second place to crude oil production, since previously there was practically no local demand for refined fuels. By looking at the evolution of crude oil production and refining in Brazil (see Table 3.2), one sees that after 1955, with the creation of Petrobas, imports of refined oil started to decrease. After forming around 95 per cent of total consumption, they gradually gave way to national products, which matched the total of the country's needs by 1969. Meanwhile, crude oil imports were increasing, and despite the increase in national production since 1958, the part played by imported crude oil still remains quite important, around one-third of the total production.

The accepted strategy concentrating on the refining industry while waiting for growth of national production of crude oil was successful. The sale of profitable refined products gave Petrobas the financial resources necessary to intensify the search and development of new oilfields. It is important to remember that the success of this policy hinged upon the existence of free movement of capital and goods within the international economy, which allowed the supply of crude oil – at a very low cost. Until the first oil crisis, importers of oil profited greatly from these low prices.

Table 3.2 Brazil: oil balance of trade (selected years)

	Crude oil production	Importation	Production	Oil products importation	Consumption
1950	339	81	527	32,269	32,933
1955	2,022	25,931	24,645	38,279	65,709
1958	18,923	33,683	48,618	30,505	80,347
1959	23,590	31,756	54,055	27,220	83,941
1963	35,710	74,441	108,684	10,011	116,996
1965	34,340	77,772	108,636	7,013	120,704
1969	63,964	110,000	152,000	—	174,121

Petrobas was able to cover occasional operational deficits mainly thanks to a tax on fuel and lubricants, in addition to funds from the national budget. It would be wrong to imagine that independent decision making in the National Oil Board and Petrobas was synonymous with total autonomy. Increased independence could only be achieved thanks to an international market through which Brazil obtained the necessary equipment and technology, which it lacked.

Even the most passionate nationalists admitted that at the time of the creation of the National Oil Board 'Quite apart from the difficulty of finance, it was impossible to import equipment' (Jesus Soares Ferriera). It was the time of war, but later, with the situation returning to normal, Brazil had to rely on foreign markets. Various legal measures exempting oil-related technology from import taxes (Act 2004/1953 Decree 37804/1955, Act 4287/1963 etc.) are evidence of the necessity to support oil production using foreign machinery. There was certainly a continuing effort to bring the technology under national control between 1955 and 1979, when refining was paramount, the proportion of domestic equipment used rose from 10 per cent to 80 per cent. Later, however, as the emphasis changed towards crude production, the proportion fell to 40 per cent and has increased only slightly since.

Despite these efforts, dependence on imported oil remained high in many countries, which felt the full dramatic consequences during the petrol crises of 1973 and 1979. But that is beyond the context of this study. What has been attempted here is to underline the importance of an open world market, and of international co-operation to find solutions to the problems faced by oil-producing South American countries. This must surely hold true not only in the context of oil, but for a whole range of problems, economic and otherwise, being faced by the nations of the South American continent.

Notes

1 Throughout the world, the oil consumption was low at this time: it represented 3.5 per cent of the consumption of energy in 1900 and 14.5 per cent in 1930. The proportion closely follows the pattern of economic development.

2 In spite of this, by the mid-1960s foreign companies controlled 84 per cent of crude oil production, 50 per cent of the refining industry and 51 per cent of oil sales in Latin America – figures due in large part to the situation in Venezuela.

3 The State controlled all crude production in Bolivia, Brazil, Chile, Cuba and Mexico by 1972; 99 per cent in Argentina; 29 per cent in Peru and 18 per cent in Colombia.

4 Oil consumption in Latin America increased by 381 per cent between 1948 and 1972.

5 Crude oil exports in six countries (Argentina, Bolivia, Colombia, Ecuador, Peru and Venezuela) rose from 111 million tonnes in 1955 to 253 million tonnes in 1970 (including 128 million tonnes in Venezuela).

6 The refining capacity in Latin America in 1969 was ten times higher than in 1940. A universal phenomenon: Trade in crude oil increased fivefold between 1950 and 1972, whereas trade in refined oil increased less than threefold.

7 Amongst Brazilian literature from that period we find some eloquent titles: 'The oil war', 'The story of a conspiracy', 'The Brazilian oil scandal', 'Oil-salvation or damnation for Brazil', 'Oil-development or slavery', etc.

8 In 1940, oil accounted for 10.5 per cent of total energy in Brazil rising to 16.6 per cent by 1947 and reaching 37.6 per cent in 1965. Consumption of oil increased more than sixteen-fold between 1945 and 1970, about 12 per cent per year, whereas the population rose by 3 per cent per year. The industrial use of oil products in 1963 was 270 times higher than in 1939.

9 Fuel oil consumed by the domestic haulage industry increased by 251 per cent between 1950 and 1965. In 1965, 68 per cent of goods were transported by road. Rail and coastal freight also accounted for a large part of this figure.

10 The theory put forward here, which I first proposed in 1971 and later expounded, seems to be recognized by Frederic Mauro.

11 The 'political' story of oil in that period is very well documented by John D. Wirth. The 1930s saw the break with the liberalism which until then had dominated world thinking with regard to oil (Martin).

12 In 1963, there existed seven refineries of which five were privately run and of the total of 306.5 million barrels produced per day, 152,000 came from the two State-owned refineries.

Bibliography

Carvalho, E. de, *O Drama da Descoberta do Petróleo Brasileiro*, Sao Paulo, Brasiliense, 1958.

Ferreira, J. S., *Petróleo, Energia Eléctrica, Siderurgia*, Rio de Janeiro, Paz e Terra, 1975.

Jacoby, N. H., *Multinational Oil*, New York, Macmillan, 1974.

Lesourd, J. A. and Gerard, C., *História Econômica–Sêculos XIX e XX*, Lisboa Classica, 1963.

Martin, J. M., *Processus D'industrialisation et dévolopement économique*, Paris, IHEAL, 1966.

Mauro, F., *Historia Econômica Mundial 1970–1970*, Rio de Janeiro, Zahar, 1973.

Mosconi, E., *La Batalla del Petróleo*, Beunos Aires, Problemas Nacionales 1957.

Peach, W. W. and Constantin, J. A., *World Resources and Industries*, New York, Harper-Row, 1972.

'Petróleo na América Latina', in *A Economia Brasileira e suas Perspectivas*, Rio de Janeiro, APEC, VI, 1967.

Smith, P. S., *Petróleo e Política no Brasil Moderno*, Rio de Janeiro, Artenova, 1978.

de la Pe a Suarez, J. L., *El Petróleo en Hispanoamerica*, Madrid, Cultura Hispanica, 1953.

Wirth, J. D., *A Politica do Desenvolvimento na Era de Vargas*, Rio de Janeiro, FGV, 1973.

Chapter four

World energy crisis and the Middle East

Dr R. Andreasjan, Institute of Oriental Studies, USSR

By energy crisis we understand a long-term set of interconnected and interdependent phenomena. It was most vividly manifested in 1973–4 and 1978–80, when two things occurred: shortage of oil supply and an explosive rise of oil prices in the world capitalist market. At the same time, shortage of a commodity in the market and the rise of its price is not called crisis by Marxists. Marxist science started to make use of the term 'energy crisis', originated in the West, applying it to one of the structural crises of contemporary capitalism, which began at the turn of the 1970s, alongside the financial and food crises.

In our opinion, the energy crisis is manifested in a sharp displacement of market price proportions in favour of oil, in the collapse of the colonial monopoly system of supplying the capitalist centres with fuel from the periphery, in the restoration of the sovereignty of the emerging independent countries over their natural resources and their independent policy in the disposal of the resources in the world market. It involved the growth of the dependence of the developed capitalist countries on the oil supplies from the newly liberated countries, and the steady rise of production costs of oil fuel in the process of drawing offshore and subpolar oilfields and of deeper producing strata into the economic turnover. The big rise of the oil prices resulted in the emergence of substantially new processes in world economy: saving of energy, especially of oil; structural shifts in the input and output parts of the energy balance due to the reduction of the share of oil; the beginning of a transition to a large scale development of renewable sources of energy, including nuclear as a long-term prospect; and the general slowing down of the rates of energy consumption.

Therefore, the energy crisis, taken in a broad context, still continues, despite the fact that following two outbreaks of oil shortages with price rises in the mid-1970s and in the first half of the present decade supply exceeds demand and there is a surplus of the commodity in the market.

Moreover, the energy crisis, as Soviet Academician Ye.M. Primakov rightly comments, affected the capitalist economy as a result 'of the coincidence in time of two processes: the production of primary energy resources lagging behind their consumption, and the liquidation of the omnipotence of the International Oil Cartel'. The crisis was the 'result of the private capitalist nature of the organization of production and sale of oil products, as well as of the crisis of neo-colonialism'.[1] Thus the crisis was brought about by contradictions in the sphere of the productive forces and relations of production at the level of the world capitalist economy in general. The energy crisis dealt heavy blows at the economies of the developed capitalist countries, but especially at the newly independent oil importing countries.

As regards the world socialist economy, it was less affected by the energy crisis because it is self-sufficient in energy supplies, principally due to the Soviet Union. The USSR not only fully provides itself with all energy resources, but satisfies also 75–90 per cent of the oil needs of its partners in the Council for Mutual Economic Co-operation (without Romania). On the other hand, the necessity to import even a minor quantity of oil from the capitalist world and the general rise of the price of this commodity have, no doubt, created no small difficulties for the implementation of the economic development plans of the East European countries.

Despite the oil shortage being felt in the world market only as late as the early 1970s, the fears of a forthcoming exhaustion of its resources were mooted in the West as early as the beginning of the present century. Every subsequent decade up to the 1970s, saw scientists and, to a greater extent, journalists expressing such alarmist views. The assertions about the quickly forthcoming exhaustion of the US oil reserves had preceded the breakthrough of American oil monopolies into the Arab countries in the 1920s and 1930s and served as a theoretical foundation for such actions. In 1942, American expert L. Weeks threateningly predicted that the US oil resources would be exhausted in twelve years.[2] That was followed by a powerful wave of American oil expansion in the Arab countries, and again, after the overthrow of the M. Mussadiq government in 1953 in Iran. In 1971, leading American newspapers asserted that the threat of a coming energy famine required a sparing use of oil and a rise in its price.

According to American statistics, the proved oil reserves in the US territory increase (in billion tons) from 2.1 in 1938 to 3.7 in 1950 and 6.0 in 1971 and then registered a gradual decrease to 3.7 in 1984, despite regular new discoveries and actual conservation of production in recent years at the level of 420–430 million tons (without the natural gas liquids).[3] Meanwhile, the well-known American geologist W. Hallbuty believes that the US oil potential is sufficient for large-scale extraction for many years of the twenty-first century.[4] In 1974, experts of the US Administration came to the conclusion that oil production in the United States might be brought up to the annual level of 1 billion tons and it would be possible to reduce imports to zero in case the oil price reached the figure of $11 per barrel (at 1973 prices).[5] A Soviet estimate places the US recoverable reserves of oil and condensate at 36 billion tons.[6]

Thus, the United States intentionally restricts oil production in its own territory in order to preserve its stocks as a strategic reserve, preferring to import it from other countries even at high prices because the domestic prices of oil products are even higher, and to assure the monopolies sufficiently big profits. All countries have, certainly, the right to their own energy supplies strategy. But the Carter and Reagan administrations declared the oil-bearing regions of the Middle East to be a sphere of US 'vital interests', though the imports from the Gulf region supplied no more than 15 per cent of American domestic consumption even at the end of the 1970s and do not exceed 5 per cent at present.[7]

What are the real oil resources of the capitalist world and to what extent do they meet the current and future consumption? According to the estimates of Soviet geologist M. Modelevsky, active or current recoverable reserves, which may be profitably extracted at the contemporary level of science, technology and market prices, amount to 190 billion tons,[8] and proved resources in 1984 were estimated by the American *Oil and Gas Journal* to be 84 billion tons.[9] This means that the proved reserves of the capitalist world will last forty-three years, and the active reserves – eighty-five years. The guaranteed period increased from twenty-one years in 1950 to thirty-nine years in 1969, and after a decrease in subsequent years again increased not only because of diminishing production, but also due to the sudden growth of proved reserves by 4 billion tons in 1984.[10] Moreover, according to M. Modelevsky, the oil requirements of the capitalist world in the period up to the year 2000 can be met by the cheapest part of the oil resources with production costs at less than $12 per ton at 1983 prices.

These favourable prospects are also ensured by positive shifts in the structure of the fuel-energy balance. From the second half of the nineteenth century to the end of the First World War, there was an increase in the share of coal which grew from 24.7 per cent in 1860 to 64.4 per cent in 1920. At the same time, the invention of the internal combustion engine on the eve of the twentieth century led to a rapid growth of oil consumption, and oil, due to its low price lasting till the early 1970s, steadily forced out coal: its share of the fuel-energy balance increased from 2.3 per cent in 1900 to 14.0 per cent in 1940, 27 per cent in 1950 and finally, to 43 per cent in 1970, when it became the leading energy source throughout the world. The capitalist world crossed that line earlier – in the early 1960s. In 1970 oil already accounted for 49 per cent of consumption of the developed industrial capitalist countries, and natural gas added, the figure was 71 per cent.[11]

But this position of oil corresponded neither to the structure of the fossil energy resources, nor to the steeply risen oil price which made it less competitive compared to coal and natural gas in a number of sectors of the economy, in that of fuel oil, in the first place. According to our calculations made on the basis of various Western and Soviet estimates (Academician V. Kirillin, 1974), oil accounts for about 10 per cent of the total recoverable reserves of industrial energy sources in coal equivalent and gas – for about 13 per cent, while the coal reserves at the present level of production may last 2000 years, i.e. they are practically inexhaustible.[12] As a result of various energy saving measures and the partial substitution of oil's old competitors, coal and gas, and new energy source – atomic power for oil, the share of the latter in the fuel-energy balance has been reduced: in its output part in 1980–2 from 44.1 per cent to 41.2 per cent in the entire world, from 48.7 per cent to 45.4 per cent in the developed capitalist world, from 41.3 per cent to 40.7 per cent in the United States, from 53.2 per cent to 49.9 per cent (in 1984 to 46 per cent or 47 per cent) in Western Europe and from 69.6 per cent to 60.9 per cent in Japan.[13]

Despite the trend noted above, oil, according to competent experts and the World Energy Conference (WEC-12, 1983), will remain a leading energy resource at least up to the year 2000, when its share of world consumption will still be 34 per cent, the share of coal being 30 per cent and of gas, 19 per cent.[14] These prospects reflect the general inertia of the fuel-energy complex, the difficulty of oil substitution in transportation and a number of industries and public utilities, the complexity and long duration of the process of the development and large-scale introduction of new energy intensive equipment, and the high costs of the production of liquid synthetic fuels from coal, tar sands and oil shales.

The necessary oil reserves are also ensured by the slowing down of the growth rate of all energy consumption. In the first half of the current century it grew relatively slowly in the world and increased 2.5 times in the period of 1900–50, but a new similar growth

(2.7 times) required only 20 years – from 1950 to 1970. For the group of developed capitalist countries the growth was 1.7 times in the 1960s alone.[15] The consumption of oil increased even more rapidly. While the annual average growth rates of energy consumption in the capitalist world in 1900–38 were 2.1 per cent, in 1950–68 they reached the figure of 3.1 per cent, and were 7.3 per cent for oil. The absolute increase of oil consumption (in million coal equivalent tons) was from 611 to 2,454, i.e. four times, and the same applies to the developed part of the capitalist world (from 537 to 2,104).[16] These rates exceeded similar indices of the gross domestic product.

After the sharp rise of oil prices, energy consumption in the 1970s grew only by 12 per cent, and in the early 1980s its growth almost stopped.[17] WEC-11 (1980) forecast the doubling of energy consumption in the world (from 8.6 to 18 billion coal equivalent tons) over a long period of 20 years, but these estimates require to be lowered.[18]

The present-day trends reveal the economically irrational structure of the energy balance on the eve of the energy crisis and the clearly too rapid tempo of oil use. In their turn, these negative processes and phenomena were a direct result of the intentionally understated oil prices, which led to its wasteful use and the growth of the dependence of the economies of many countries of the capitalist world on the import of that energy resource. At the same time, the oil production in a number of Western countries, the United States in the first place, was artificially restricted. In his State of the Union Message to the Congress in January, 1975, President Nixon admitted that in the 1970s the United States had lost its 'surplus energy potential', which it had possessed in the 1960s.[19]

The gap between the level of energy consumption and the possibilities of its satisfaction by one's own sources grew in Western states and Japan. The production of primary energy resources in Western Europe increased in 1961–71 to 4 per cent, and their use – by 63 per cent. The share of imports in the domestic energy consumption rose in these years in the developed capitalist countries from 20 to 33 per cent; in the United States from 7 to 11 per cent, in Western Europe from 37 to 65 per cent, in Japan from 55 to 98 per cent.[20] The import of oil by Western Europe in the period of 1950–72 increased 17.5 times, and by Japan 180 times. The United States stopped being an oil exporter and became a big importer of oil, the import of which increased nine times.[21] At the same time, the share of that group of countries of the proved oil reserves was only 11 per cent, while in 1938 it was the biggest –

64 per cent.[22] After the Second World War the centre of gravity in this sphere definitely shifted to the group of developing countries. Thus, the centre of capitalism found itself seriously dependent for energy on the developing countries who have been and are waging a stubborn struggle against neo-colonial exploitation, for the consolidation of their political sovereignty and economic independence.

Despite this, the oil monopolies of the West continued to pursue the course of expanding the supply of cheap oil from their concessions in Asia, Africa and Latin America to the markets of the developed capitalist states. Low energy prices made it possible for these states to save greatly floating capital and to make investments firstly in the manufacturing industries, to develop advanced science-intensive branches, to enlarge the scientific and technological gap between them and the former colonies and semi-colonies, to perpetuate the latter's position as a backward, unequal and dependent part of the world capitalist economy, and to intensify their exploitation. The developed capitalist world to no small extent owes its considerable economic growth in the first post-war decades to cheap oil. With its help the 'Seven Sisters' have stifled the West European coal industry.

Why did the 'Seven Sisters' sell oil to consumers at low prices without suffering losses? They not only incurred no losses, but made big profits. First, there was the extremely low cost of production of the concessions, much lower than that in the United States. In the late 1960s the production cost of one barrel of oil in the Persian Gulf area was 10 cents, while in the United States it was on the average $1.7.[23] Even at the end of the 1970s the capital cost per unit of production capacity of oil was seventy-three times less than in the United States and 8.8 times less than in Western Europe.[24]

The second cause was the essentially colonial and monopolistic mechanism of exploitation of cheap oil resources at the concessions, imposed by imperialism. The concessions were obtained by putting pressure on the respective countries, their terms having placed huge territories at the full disposal of the Western companies for the period till the end of the century. The concessionaires themselves determined the scale of prospecting and production of oil, and the directions of its import. Concessionary payments were so small – 25 cents per barrel in 1948 – that it made it profitable to sell oil even at low monopoly prices. But when countries of Latin America and afterwards the Middle East had obtained an official fifty-fifty share of income from oil production, monopolies brought the price down to a very low level so as to pay less to governments of the above-mentioned countries. In 1970, the official price of the Arabian light was only $1.8 per barrel (or, in fact, $1.4, if allowances are taken into account), i.e. almost twenty to twenty-three times lower than in 1982 (in current prices).[25] In 1970 the share of OPEC members' income in the average price of petrol in the West European market was no more than 6 per cent, that of the concessionaires 42 per cent, and of the governments of the importing countries 52 per cent.[26] It amounted to actual robbery of the principal and unrenewable wealth of the oil-producing countries of the East and Latin America. The profits of the monopolies on the capital invested in the Gulf countries in 1971 were 125 per cent, while in the United States in 1972 they were 8.7 per cent.[27] To perpetuate such conditions, monopolies and their governments stopped at nothing in interfering with the home affairs of the Middle East governments.

Finally, the third cause was the use by the monopolies of their vertical structure comprising the entire chain of operations, from prospecting to sale, with the control of the old cartel over the main markets. Under such conditions the oil export prices came to be an intra-firm transfer, allowing for the accountancy of the incomes of the producing subsidiaries. Value added was as a result of transportation and processing and the product was sold in the market at a price ten times higher than the oil price.[28] These prices, too, were not high and at the same time enabled the members of the cartel to receive huge super profits with the low monopoly price of the raw material.

The monopolies received the bulk of their profits by exploiting the oil riches of the Middle East, or, to be more exact, of the Persian Gulf area. With the help of Arab and Iranian oil they made the West and Japan directly dependent on their operations, imposed on them an inordinately high place of oil in energy consumption and thus were enormously enriched. The share of that region in the proved oil reserves of the capitalist world rose from 20 per cent before the Second World War to almost 50 per cent by 1950 – two-thirds excluding the United States – and 69 per cent by 1960.[29] Oil production in that region grew much faster than in the entire capitalist world: the respective rates of growth, in 1950–79, were according to our estimates, 19 and 5 per cent. The share of the region in the total oil production of the capitalist world increased from 6.6 per cent in 1938 to 18 per cent in 1950, 36.8 per cent in 1970 and 49 per cent in 1977, and as regards export, it rose in the same years from 10.8 per cent to 37.8 per cent, 56.8 per cent and, finally, 68.5 per cent in 1976.[30] Thus, the Middle East became the main oil arsenal and centre of the profitability of the entire capitalist world. In 1970 Iran and the Arab countries of the Middle East and North Africa supplied up to four-fifths of the oil import requirements of Western Europe, two fifths of those of the United

States. In the same year, according to our estimates, more than one-half of the total oil output was produced by the American 'Seven Sisters' and a number of US independent firms; the BP and Shell produced two times less, and the rest went to French, other Western and Japanese capital.

Meanwhile, at the beginning of the 1970s, it became clear that there appeared an acute contradiction between the system of low oil prices and reality. The oil monopolies became interested in an oil price rise because of widely spread inflation which crossed national borders and entered world markets, because of the new opportunity to develop newly discovered big oil reserves in the North Sea and Alaska at high production costs (which was also in accordance with the plans of the governments of the United States and Great Britain), tighter controls over coal companies, development of nuclear power and, finally, increased taxation of OPEC members. In their turn, the latter also strove not only to increase national participation in the development of their oil industry and the taxation of the concessionary firms, but to obtain a rise of the artificially understated oil prices. All these processes took place against the background of a simultaneous cyclic revival of the capitalist economy in the early 1970s, when it was difficult to satisfy the sharply increased demand for oil through the existing production capacities. Not wishing to be responsible for such an unpopular measure as an oil price rise, the members of the cartel decided to put the burden on OPEC and therefore, on the one hand, feigned resistance to OPEC's demands and on the other hand, declared that they are forced to raise prices in response to the pressure of 'avaricious Arabs and Persians' as has been noted by many authors.[31] To increase pressure on their governments and to get their permission for an oil price rise, the members of the oil cartel intensified tension in the market and created an artificial shortage of fuel in the winter of 1972–3.

In October 1973, during the course of the fourth Arab-Israeli war, Arab countries and OPEC, in order to put pressure on the accomplices of Zionism, curtailed oil production and even introduced an embargo on deliveries to the United States and certain other Western countries. Under these conditions OPEC unilaterally announced a series of oil price rises, and in January 1974 brought it to the level of $11.65 per barrel. It is important to note that the embargo was of a short duration, and the cut of production was small. The oil monopolies used this decision of the Arab countries to cut down their supplies to the market thus creating a shortage of oil for the consumers. The overall shortage of energy in the first quarter of 1974 was, according to R. Stobaugh, 5 per cent in the

United States and 12 per cent in Western Europe.[32] Thus the first outbreak of the energy crisis occurred in the capitalist world.

The second outbreak occurred in 1979–80. In between the United States, reassured by the failure of the Arab oil embargo and facing the unwillingness of the American monopolies to increase investments in the development of the indigenous oil production while governmental control over the level of oil prices was maintained, continued to expand their fuel imports. In 1978, the share of the imported oil and oil products in the United States domestic consumption reached 52 per cent,[33] in 1977 the share of the Arab countries in the oil imports was 47 per cent and in consumption, 21 per cent.[34] By 1979, according to OECD estimates, inflation caused the real price of oil to come down as compared with 1974, by 17 per cent,[35] which dealt a heavy blow not only to OPEC, but also to the old cartel whose real aggregate profits became 30 per cent less in the same period, according to the London *Economist*.[36] Simultaneously it became clear that the development of alternative sources of energy, an important integral part of governmental programmes, proved impossible at the existing price level, as the costs were much higher. Again the 'Seven Sisters' were keenly interested in raising oil prices.

To do so they utilized the cessation of Iranian oil supplies to the United States after the 1978–9 revolution, though this oil accounted only for 5 per cent in the US imports, and Saudi Arabia, on the insistent request of the Americans, increased its production and compensated the curtailed commodity deliveries from Iran. Consequently, there was no real oil shortage in the market. But American monopolies in the summer of 1979 once again created an artificial shortage of oil products in the US domestic market. At that time the American administration started to subsidize its companies in order to buy fuel oil and diesel oil in Western Europe, which, in turn, created an oil shortage there, too. Brokers' companies in the Rotterdam spot market immediately raised the prices four times. Monopolies purchasing oil from OPEC members at prices established by long-term contracts, set out to sell it at the spot market prices. Under such conditions OPEC members, not wishing to be robbed, raised their contractual prices, till in 1982 the price of the Arabian crude reached the figure of $32 per barrel.

Thus this time too, the energy crisis was brought about by the monopolies, but the fault was again laid by most Western mass media on OPEC. Characteristically, the monopolies shifted the burden of the rise in purchasing prices on to the consumers, having raised the prices on oil products and shown a great increase of their profits exactly in 1974–5 and 1979–80. Of course, the income of

OPEC members from oil also grew several times. Nevertheless, it should be noted that despite the superficial community of commercial interests of the members of the old Western cartel and of the new cartel of the developing nations, the former strive to get super profits in the interests of a handful of their shareholders, and the latter to do away with neo-colonial exploitation and to develop their national economies which to a very great measure depended on a single exhaustible resource. OPEC raised the oil prices up to the economically justified level of purchasing power, but it actually was able to do this only, when it was profitable to certain influential Western circles.

The energy crisis had many, sometimes contradictory effects. In the conditions of that crisis OPEC members did away with the system of concessions, restored national sovereignty over their natural resources, proved able to raise the nominal oil prices almost twenty times and real prices, according to our estimates, 6.6 times, made big investments in the development of national economy, and an important step on the way to industrialization; they started to create the basis of an economy which is less dependent on the sale of one single commodity. Iraq and Iran also went along this path but their senseless and cruel war has dealt such a heavy blow to their economies that a number of years will be necessary for rehabilitation. The accumulation of big incomes from oil when the absorbtive capacity of the economy is limited, enabled the oil exporting countries of the Gulf region to form a new group of big exporters of capital, which substantially improved their positions in the capitalist world.

On the other hand, the negative impact on the position of the Gulf region in the world economy, in the oil market in the first place, was produced by such factors as measures implemented by the West to save oil and to weaken its position in the energy balance; the creation of huge commercial stocks of oil was used to put pressure on OPEC; the attempts by Great Britain and Norway to seize the growing markets in 1983–5; the strengthening of the position of outsiders in the oil market; and finally, the economic crisis of the early 1980s and its consequences. As a result, while the share of the region in the proved reserves of the capitalist world was about 64.5 per cent in 1984, its share of production after 1978 has been steadily decreasing coming down to 31.5 per cent in 1984. Production returned to the level of the second half of the 1960s, and the same trends exist in exports: since 1976 the share of the Middle East has come down to 48.4 per cent in 1984.[37] In 1983 the income of the Arab members of OPEC was only one-half of that of 1980.[38] The balance of current accounts of all countries' members of the OPEC decreased from $+114$ billion dollars in 1980 to -27 billion dollars in 1983.[39] The size of their investments abroad also diminished. The external debt of the entire Arab world, including trade debts, increased substantially. There was a curtailment of common investment programmes and the rates of development came down sharply.

At the same time, the preservation of oil as the principal energy source and the interest of a number of Western powers in maintaining a high oil price level guarantees the irreversibility of the changes in the exchange proportions in favour of oil.

The oil price rise negatively affected the developing oil importing countries, the more so, as the share of oil in their energy balance is much higher than in the West (up to two-thirds). The energy crisis coincided with tempestuous inflation, their indebtedness to the centres of capitalism grew at a quick pace. The Western powers in the conditions of an economic crisis adopted the policy of 'new protectionism', restricting the exports of the emerging free countries. The economic assistance by the OPEC members, nine-tenths of which has been provided by the Arab oil monarchies, makes the position of oil importers a bit easier, but, first, it is far from compensating their losses, and, second, this assistance has been greatly reduced.

Repeated oil price rises were a factor which worsened the conditions of reproduction at the centres of capitalism, led to a two times reduction of the rates of economic development of the industrial capitalist countries, and played a certain role in the biggest and longest economic crises of contemporary capitalism after the Second World War. At the same time, the rising prices on the leading energy resource brought about positive shifts: the reduction of the resource intensity of the GDP, creation of a more rational structure of the energy balance, and an important scientific and technological progress in all branches of economy. But even these positive factors are, of course, unable to free the capitalist world and its centre from new economic crises and improve the very modest general growth rates (with crises taken into account) of the gross domestic product, forecast both in the West and in USSR at any rate for the period up to the mid-1990s.

Notes

1 Ye. M. Primakov. *The East after the Collapse of the Colonial System* (Moscow, 1982): 135, 142 (in Russian).
2 S. M. Lisichkin. *World's Energy Resources* (Moscow, 1977): 14 (in Russian).

3 *Oil and Gas Journal* (last issues of the respective years).

4 *Wall Street Journal*, 27 January, 1980.

5 *Energy Future*, Report of the Energy Project of the Harvard Business School, edited by Robert Stobaugh and Daniel Yergen (New York, 1979): 46.

6 *Cadastre of Foreign Countries Possessing Oil and Natural Gas Resources* (London, 1983), Vol. 2: 225 (in Russian).

7 Calculated according to data in *OAPEC Bulletin*, 28 February, 1984; *The Petroleum Economist*, December, 1983: 452; *Platt's Oilgram Price Report*, 6 April, 1984.

8 *Oil and Gas Resources and Prospects of their Development*, editor-in-chief M. Modelevsky (Moscow, 1983): 37 (in Russian).

9 *Oil and Gas Journal*, 28 December, 1984.

10 Calculated according to data in: *Oil and Gas Industry of Foreign Countries (1938–1978)*, statistical reference book, edited by M. S. Modelevsky (Moscow, 1983) (in Russian).

11 S. M. Lisichkin. Op. cit.: 9; *Oil and Gas Industry* . . .: 8 (in Russian).

12 Calculated according to data in S. M. Lisichkin, Op. cit.: 6–7 (in Russian).

13 Calculated according to data in *Yearbook of World Energy Statistics* (1983) UN., New York; *BP Statistical Yearbook of World Energy* (London, 1984).

14 A. A. Beschinsky, 'Problems of development of world energy, *Teploenergetika* (Moscow, 1984), No. 3: 6 (in Russian).

15 Calculated according to data in S. M. Lisichkin, Op. cit.: 7; *Oil and Gas Industry* . . .: 8–9 (in Russian).

16 *Energy Crisis in the Capitalist World*: 9–10; R. N. Andreasjan, A. D. Kaziukov, *OPEC in the World of Oil* (Moscow, 1978): 154 (in Russian).

17 Calulated according to data in *Yearbook of World Energy Statistics* (UN, New York, 1983) No. 4.

18 A. A. Beschinsky, Yu. M. Kogan. *Economic Problems of Electrification* (Moscow, 1983): 134 (in Russian).

19 *Energy Crisis in the Capitalist World*: 17 (in Russian).

20 *World Energy Supplies* (1973) tables 1, 2.

21 Ye. M. Primakov. 'Energy crisis, in *Deepening of the General Crisis of Capitalism* (Moscow, 1976): 198 (in Russian).

22 Calculated according to data in *Oil and Gas Industry* . . .: 77–86 (in Russian).

23 L. M. Tomashpolsky, *Oil and Gas in World Energy Balance (1900–2000)* (Moscow, 1968): 49 (in Russian).

24 Calculated according to data in *Capital Investments of the World Petroleum Industry 1978* (New York, Chase Manhattan Bank, 1979): 12–13; *BP Statistical Review of World Energy, 1982* (London, 1983): 18, 26.

25 *Oil and Gas Industry* . . .: 209 (in Russian).

26 ibid.: 222.

27 R. N. Andreasjan, 'Oil and anti-imperialist struggle', *The Communist* (1974) No. 5: 102 (in Russian).

28 *Oil and Gas Industry* . . .: 227 (in Russian).

29 ibid.: 77–86.

30 Calculated according to data in *Oil and Gas Industry* . . .: 115–20; 'Conjuncture of capitalist economy and main commodity markets in 1980–85', *Supplements to the Bulletin of Foreign Commercial Information (BIKI)* (in Russian).

31 J. M. Blair, *The Control of Oil*, (London, 1977); A. Sampson, *The Seven Sisters* (London, 1976); Jean-Marie Chevalier, *Le nouvel enjeu pétroliere* (Paris, 1973); *Oil and Class Struggle*, P. Noore and L. Turner (eds) (London, 1980); *Foreign Affairs* (1976) No. 25; P. Odell, *Oil and World Power* (Baltimore, 1978).

32 *Energy Future* . . .: 163.

33 *Bulletin of Foreign Commercial Information (BIKI)* (1979), Supplement No. 2: 185 (in Russian).

34 Calculated according to data in *Oil Statistics. Supply and Disposal 1974–1978/79*.

35 *BIKI* (Moscow, 1979), supplement No. 2: 185, 224 (in Russian).

36 *The Economist*, 15 October (London, 1983): 83.

37 Calculated according to data in *BIKI* (Moscow, 1985), supplement No. 2: 175–9 (in Russian).

38 *BIKI*, 24 May, 1984 (in Russian); *Middle East Economic Digest*, 29 June 1984.

39 *BIKI*, 30 June 1980; *BIKI*, (Moscow, 1984), supplement No. 3: 22.

Session two

National aspects

Chapter five

Oil and the evolution of US policy towards the developing areas, 1900–1950: an essay in interpretation

Jeffry A. Frieden, Department of Political Science, University of California, Los Angeles

The 1920s and 1930s were a watershed in relations between the United States and the world's underdeveloped areas. At the outset of the period the United States exercised firm stewardship of a host of nations in and around the Caribbean, held a few colonial outposts in the Pacific and a presence in China, and was virtually invisible elsewhere. The Roosevelt Corollary to the Monroe Doctrine was in full force, with its presumption that

> brutal wrongdoing, or an impotence which results in a general loosening of the ties of civilized society, may finally require intervention by some civilized nation, and in the Western Hemisphere the United States cannot ignore this duty.[1]

By the late 1930s the American sphere of influence had expanded to include most of the Western Hemisphere, yet the Roosevelt Corollary had been expressly disavowed. US military power was exerted sparingly and the sovereignty of local rulers was generally respected. Outside the Western Hemisphere both American diplomacy and American business were well established, bordering on predominant. The seeds of the post-war era, with its American-supervised decolonization, had been sown.

This chapter examines the process by which American policy towards the underdeveloped world evolved from a pale Caribbean image of classical European imperialism to a new form of Good Neighbourliness, focusing on American oil policy, one of the most contentious areas of north–south diplomacy in the period. Its purpose is not to give an overview of American foreign oil policy in the Twentieth century, nor to unearth new primary sources, only to explore the geopolitical and economic origins of the shift in American policy. It is simply the attempt of a political scientist to examine an important analytical puzzle in US foreign policy, the shift from a form of gunboat diplomacy in which national power and private economic interest seemed to coincide, to a new pattern in which the automatic and direct diplomatic defence of private business faded and even disappeared.

The previous pattern

The prevailing American attitude before about 1925 towards those parts of Africa, Asia, and Latin America in which there was any US presence at all can fairly be characterized as assuming that the strategic interests of the United States and the economic interests of American citizens abroad were so closely linked that an attack on one immediately endangered the other. Whether strategic concerns were driven by economic interest, or economic interests guided by strategic action – whether trade followed the flag or the flag followed trade – the flag, trade, and the dollar were closely linked in the eyes of policy makers, traders, and investors.

The general extension of US military, political, and economic influence into the Caribbean region is a well-known story. Well before the Spanish-American war, there was a broad consensus among both American strategic and economic thinkers that control of the inevitable trans-isthmian canal was vitally important to the United States. Once the canal route was secured it was even more obvious that, as then-Secretary of War Elihu Root put it in 1905:

> The inevitable effect of our building the Canal must be to require us to police the surrounding premises. In the nature of things, trade and control, and the obligation to keep order which go with them, must come our way.[2]

Deeds followed words, and by the end of the First World War the Caribbean region was unquestionably a sphere of American military and economic predominance. Direct politico-military control was exercised at one time or another over Puerto Rico, Cuba, the Dominican Republic, Haiti, Nicaragua, Honduras, and of course Panama; American troops intervened twice in Mexico; and the threat of force served to cement American influence where force itself was not used.

The other underdeveloped area to which American concern extended was east Asia, especially the Philippine colony and China. Partly this was out of necessity: by 1900 most of the rest of Asia and Africa was already behind colonial walls, while South America was a nearly-unchallengeable British preserve. Partly, too, American interest in the China market was long-standing, dating back practically to the founding of the Republic. In any case, by the turn of the century the United States government was aggressively insisting upon its rights to equal access to Chinese economic opportunities, most notably in Secretary of State John Hay's famous Open Door Notes of 1899 and 1900. Here American military power was of little use, faced with the equal or superior forces of other interested powers, and US economic interests were also in most regards weaker than the European, Russian, and Japanese competitors. Yet the United States did succeed in becoming one of the crowd in China, even if it was a somewhat less equal partner than, say, Great Britain or Japan.

In this American emulation of classical European imperialism, overseas investment in petroleum was of some significance, although it was only during and after the First World War that it became a major diplomatic concern. For one thing, the US Navy did not commit itself to an oil-burning fleet until 1913; for another, American domestic oil production seemed more than sufficient until the First World War produced fears of imminent shortages. Overseas investments by US oil firms rose from $224 million in 1908 to $604 million in 1919 and $1.3 billion in 1929, going from 14 to 18 per cent of total American foreign direct investment. Before 1910 most of the foreign investment was in distribution networks: by 1919 foreign production had become important, and by 1929 some 58 per cent of American overseas oil investments were in Latin America, primarily in and around the Caribbean, while another 14 per cent were in other areas of Asia and Africa.[3]

American government policy towards petroleum paralleled its more general attitude towards the strategic centrality of overseas American economic activity. Where American oilmen were predominant and the region was deemed strategically important, as in the Caribbean, the US government aggressively defended the position of American oil investors against hostile local attackers and sought to limit or exclude rival European oilmen. Where the Europeans held the whiphand, as in the Middle East and the Dutch East Indies, the US government pushed insistently for the admission of American petroleum companies on a footing at least equal to that of the colonial power's firms.

The most important area of American petroleum activity until after the Second World War was the Caribbean region, especially Mexico and Venezuela. In this region, petroleum was included in the more general government belief that foreign (i.e. non-American) economic activities represented both a security and an economic hazard. The State Department thus championed American petroleum enterprise with great vigour. It fought what it perceived as a tilt towards British oil interests on the part of some of Mexico's revolutionary governments. In the early 1920s, it supported American oilmen in Venezuela against the Anglo-Dutch interests that originally dominated that country's petroleum. American diplomats pushed the Colombian government in the late 1920s to favour American oilmen; similar efforts were exerted in Peru and Argentina. And, in a series of 1918 notes to his chargé in Costa Rica that summarized the most extreme version of this 'Closed Door' policy, Secretary of State Lansing responded to the news that a British group was negotiating for oil exploration rights by insisting:

> [The] Department considers it most important that only approved Americans should possess oil concessions in the neighborhood of the Panama Canal. Amory concession does not appear to meet these requirements. Use best efforts to carry into effect this policy.[4]

The aggressive American policy met with extraordinary success. Between 1912 and 1922, crude oil production by American companies in the Western Hemisphere (not including the United States) went from 25,905 to 417,130 barrels per day (bpd). Just as important, the share of the American oil companies in total non-US Western Hemisphere crude production went from under 50 per cent in 1912 to over 76 per cent at its 1922 peak; the relative increase was entirely at the expense of the Anglo-Dutch companies. By the mid-1920s, however, the United States had begun to relax some of its earlier exclusionary policies, in large part in return for European agreement to open their colonial doors to some American oilmen.[5]

After the First World War, indeed, American diplomats and oilmen, concerned about the apparent depletion of American reserves, attempted to break into promising areas that were under the 'protection' of European rivals. American worries were inflamed by a string of threatening European assertions, including the impolitic remarks in 1920 of a prominent English banker that:

> America before very long will have to purchase from British companies, and to pay for in dollar currency in progressively increasing proportion, the oil she cannot do without and is no longer able to furnish from her own states. . . . With the exception of Mexico, and to lesser extent Central America, the outer world is securely barricaded against an American invasion in force. There may be small, isolated allies, but there can never be a massed attack. The British position is impregnable.[6]

The British position in the Eastern Hemisphere – along with that of the Dutch and French – might have seemed impregnable in

1920, but it was soon to be successfully challenged by the United States. The American attack on colonial and semi-colonial pre-ferences focused on the Middle East and the Netherlands East Indies.

Most of the promising oil properties of the Middle East were indeed in British hands, either as part of the territories mandated to the British by the League of Nations or as more general spheres of British influence. Throughout the region, from Palestine to Kuwait and from Mesopotamia to Persia, US oil companies found them-selves unable to operate. Despite British dissimulation on the point, there was clearly a conscious policy to reserve the region to the Anglo-Persian Oil Company and Royal Dutch Shell, with some French participation allowed. In Holland's East India colony, a similar policy of excluding American firms was pursued.

The United States government fought British, French, and Dutch exclusion of American oilmen on two fronts. First, the US govern-ment protested vigorously to the European states involved that their policies were clear violations both of generally accepted Open Door principles and of such international agreements as the League of Nations mandates and the Treaty of Sèvres, which disposed of the Ottoman Empire. The principles involved were less than clear, since the United States had been pursuing something less than an Open Door in the Western Hemisphere, and the US had refused both to join the League and to sign the Turkish peace treaty. Second, and more pointedly, the US government began refusing oil leases on federal land to firms from countries deemed 'non-reciprocating', most prominently to Royal Dutch Shell.

Under relentless American pressure, the British, French, and Dutch gradually gave way. As has been indicated, in the process the Americans relaxed some of their opposition to Anglo-Dutch oil activity in Latin America, but it was probably the more specific American pressure that forced the door open. In July 1928 the Dutch and US governments reached formal agreement on American access to the petroleum of the Netherlands East Indies. In the same month, the famous Red Line Agreement gave an American group a share of the Anglo-Dutch-French-Gulbenkian monopoly in the former Ottoman Empire. In Kuwait, Romania, Persia, and elsewhere, American oilmen were permitted some degree of access. The principled American stand on the Open Door in petroleum lasted precisely as long as it took for American oilmen to be let in. Once this aim was accomplished, the US was perfectly content to see the door slam shut.

From 1890 until the 1920s, then, the pursuit and growth of American political and economic influence in the underdeveloped world followed a more or less coherent and unified pattern to which overseas petroleum policy conformed. A strict and direct relationship was drawn by policy makers between American overseas economic and geostrategic influence. Where possible, as in the Caribbean region, the United States appropriated to itself what power and wealth was available. Where other colonial nations had beaten the Americans to the punch, as in the Middle East and the Dutch East Indies, the US government used its ample powers of persuasion to force closed doors open long enough for American oilmen to enter.

The pattern transformed

If American policy towards the underdeveloped areas up to the 1920s could be graphically represented as a smoothly rising curve, indicating ever-tightening control over such regions within the American sphere as the Caribbean and ever-deeper intrusions into such rival spheres as the Middle East, during the late 1920s and 1930s the curve began to behave in most unaccustomed ways. The United States government appeared to release its hold on areas previously within its grip, and more generally to remove itself from the business of stimulating and accompanying American private investors abroad. By no means did the State Department abandon the overseas American business community, but the levels and automaticity of mutual support and encouragement were quite drastically reduced. In petroleum diplomacy especially, the interests of American investors were disregarded in ways that could not have been predicted from earlier experience.

The process might be characterized as a fitful series of initiatives that began in the 1920s where American influence was strongest, in the Caribbean basin, and was gradually extended to the rest of Latin America, hence to the British Empire, and finally to the non-Soviet world by the end of the Second World War. The new set of policies was not implemented uniformly or without hypocrisy, nor was there a total lack of continuity between previous experience and the new look, and, as we will make clear further on, there is no implication here that the shift in policy was born out of some altruistic set of good intentions. None the less, American policy towards the underdeveloped world did change, and it is the purpose of what follows to outline the emergent course of conduct and to explain the reasons for its emergence, with special reference to petroleum.

The very important role played by Dwight Morrow, senior partner of J. P. Morgan and Company, in the evolution of

American policy in this period is both illustrative and instructive. In the early 1920s Morrow spent much of his time in Cuba on behalf of the Morgan firm, both to secure the house's investments and to work with the State Department and President Harding's Cuban representative in stabilizing the island's finances. The very powerful American investors resident in Cuba, and especially the sugar interests, were continually and insistently calling for US intervention on their behalf. Both Morrow and the presidential representative, however, argued successfully against intervention on the grounds that respect for Cuban sovereignty was a far better path to long run stability. As Morrow put it:

> Of course the Government of Cuba has been, and is, very bad. It is possible – yes, it is probable – that the United States might run Cuba much better. As I get older, however, I become more and more convinced that good government is not a substitute for self-government. The kind of mistakes that America would make in running Cuba would be different from those that the Cubans themselves make, but they would probably cause a new kind of trouble and a new kind of suffering.
>
> We ought not to use the Platt Amendment to collect the debts, or to enforce the contracts, of private individuals.[7]

Morrow got a chance to implement his views when he was appointed US Ambassador to Mexico in 1927. Morrow's three short years in Mexico left a lasting stamp on US-Mexican relations, for Morrow abandoned the more or less intransigent defence of private investors that had characterized most American diplomats in Latin America. Instead, Morrow took a flexible position, settling the long-standing oil rights dispute by recognizing for the first time Mexican sovereignty over its resources in return for legal commitments to the oil producers. In negotiations on Mexican policies towards foreign oil companies and the refunding of Mexico's defaulted debt, Morrow took Mexican nationalism as a given and attempted only to ensure general stability and co-operative relations. The famous Morrow Mission was indeed successful in restoring a measure of goodwill in US–Mexican relations, and it became a sort of a model for, as his biographer put it: 'the policy of the Great Powers in dealing with other backward but suddenly nationalistic countries'.[8]

When, in 1938, the Mexican government carried its oil policy to its more or less logical conclusion and nationalized virtually all foreign oil properties, the American response was once again measured. Protests were filed, suits brought, and some diplomatic pressure applied, but American Ambassador Josephus Daniels was anything but sympathetic to the oilmen. As Daniels wrote to Secretary of State Hull:

> I do not agree with the public man who said 'all oil stinks', but we have seen so many evil practices growing out of the greed for its possession and the power it gives that we are warned to be cautious when we are asked to further the desires of the oil interests.[9]

The 1942 accord which settled the matter was highly favourable to the Mexicans, and the oil companies considered the attitude of the US government disgraceful.

Long before the 1938 Mexican nationalization, though, the focus of US interest in Latin American oil had shifted from Mexico to Venezuela. In 1929 American oilmen had more money invested in Venezuela than in Mexico ($226 million to $205 million) and, with the Mexican industry in the throes of a secular decline, it was producing just one-third of the Venezuelan (122,345 to 376,809 barrels per day). By 1936 Mexican production had declined still further, Venezuelan production had increased, and with the crisis depressing equity values American investments in the Venezuelan oil industry were well over twice those in Mexico ($174 million to $69 million).[10]

In Venezuela, as in Mexico before it, the new US policy gradually gained and was applied. For many years the American oilmen had been on the best of terms with Venezuelan dictator Juan Vicente Gómez, who ruled from 1908 until his death in 1935. The regimes that succeeded him responded to popular pressure to punish the despot's allies and moved to tighten control of the foreign oil companies. When in fact successive Venezuelan governments in the late 1930s and 1940s began to press for a larger share of petroleum revenues, the oilmen were shocked and chagrined to find the US government arrayed against them and on the side of the Venezuelans.

The charge against the American petroleum firms was led initially, within the State Department, by American minister to Venezuela Meredith Nicholson, appointed in 1935. Nicholson told Washington that the American oilmen in Venezuela were of the 'old school of imperialists' who believed that American military force 'ought logically to follow American investments in foreign countries wherever required by the interests involved'. The petroleum executives had, with their blind support for the hated Gómez regime, followed 'a policy of shortsightedness verging on stupidity', and they were simply 'reaping the fruits of what they had so misguidedly sown'.[11]

Nicholson's contempt for the oilmen was seconded by Lawrence Duggan, head of the State Department's Division of American Republics. Duggan fought tenaciously, in both the Mexican and Venezuelan cases, for a more flexible policy towards Latin nationalism. Telling his superiors in 1939 that the oilmen had in Venezuela been 'arbitrary, high-handed, insensitive, and ruthless', he said of the oilmen:

> It must not be permitted them (as occurred in the case of the Mexican dispute) to jeopardize our entire good neighbour policy through obstinacy and short-sightedness. Our national interests as a whole far outweigh those of the petroleum companies.[12]

Duggan and the new line triumphed in Venezuela as they did elsewhere in Latin America. In the Venezuelan case, the shift culminated in US government support for a new oil law that gave the host government a far greater share of petroleum revenues than had ever been conceded by American oil interests. With the advice of official and unofficial American representatives, the Venezuelans extracted from the companies a new formula for profit-sharing, a fifty-fifty division of petroleum earnings. This nearly doubled the Venezuelan share of oil revenue, and the Venezuelan formula became a standard in profit-splitting accords between American oil companies and host governments.

In the Middle East major changes in US government policy also took place in the 1940s. The level of interest had been lower than in the Caribbean, partly because the immense potential for petroleum development in the area did not become clear until around the time of the Second World War – in the late 1930s Venezuelan production was about double that of the entire Middle East – and partly because American firms controlled only a small fraction of the region's petroleum resources. The Second World War, however, stimulated unprecedented US government concern over the fate of Persian Gulf oil. Secretary of the Navy James Forrestal highlighted the general importance of the area's petroleum in a 1944 letter to Secretary of State Stettinius:

> The prestige and hence the influence of the United States is in part related to the wealth of the Government and its nationals in terms of oil resources, foreign as well as domestic.

With negotiations over the post-war settlement on his mind, Forrestal noted that 'the bargaining power of the United States in international conferences . . . will depend in some degree upon the retention by the United States of such . . . resources'.[13]

Yet, much as in the Western Hemisphere, the US government

ended up entrusting oil development to negotiations between private firms and the host countries themselves. When the government intervened it was not to force local acceptance of the companies' demands, but usually to smooth the way to negotiations between firms and host nations. The process was complex, protracted, and mired in domestic infighting within the United States, but by 1945 or so the State Department had begun to settle upon a Middle Eastern oil policy that would last nearly thirty years. American (and other) international oil companies would co-operate in the development of the region's plentiful petroleum, with the tacit support of the United States and on the understanding that good relations with the local governments were of extraordinary importance. By 1948 the old Red Line Agreement had been voided. In 1950 the oil companies, under State Department pressure, agreed to a Venezuela-style fifty-fifty split of oil profits with the Saudi regime, and indeed before long such agreements were the Persian Gulf norm. American firms got access to the area's oil-fields; American diplomats were glad to see the finances of the region's conservative rulers stabilized, and, of course, the rulers themselves were quite satisfied with the arrangement. Here, too, the old oil diplomacy of imperial intrigue and subversion had been supplanted by more regular ties between host and home governments and firms.

In both Latin American and the Middle East, then, American policy was fundamentally transformed in the interwar years. The pre-existing patterns of gunboat diplomacy, forceful and often expansionist government defence of private interests, and aggressive diplomatic promotion of the extension of US economic influence were gradually discarded. No longer would policy makers and businessmen assume an identity of purpose. American policy became far more subtle, cognizant of conditions in the developing world, willing to compromise with local leaders.

The transformation interpreted

This brief survey of well-known developments in US policy towards the petroleum of the underdeveloped areas from the 1890s until the 1940s serves only as a prelude to a more controversial task: explaining the sources of change in US policy. The necessarily brief discussion that follows will undoubtedly lose the richness of detail in its attempt to narrow the range of factors regarded as causal. None the less, it is both necessary and possible to draw some analytical conclusions concerning the events discussed above.

We can first dispose of two popular explanations of the shift in policy: American ideology and American party politics. The evidence examined here provides little or no support for an emphasis on the power of the Open Door idea as a motive in America's international behaviour. In the Caribbean from the Spanish-American war until the 1930s, the door was most emphatically closed to European competition. In the Middle East in the 1920s, American pressure forced colonial exclusion to be dropped only long enough to permit a few US petroleum firms entry. In a few areas, such as China, the Open Door was followed with some coherence (although even there the received wisdom receives less than firm support from historians). Nor does a more general 'liberal' ideology seem to have mattered much either in the first phase of American expansion or in the new age that might be dated to the Morrow Mission. Neither set of policies was motivated by some general belief in the magic of the market place; both tolerated and even encouraged (very different kinds of) government intervention in economic affairs.

Party politics also provides little or no explanatory assistance. The Roosevelt administration's policies toward oil in the Caribbean and the Middle East, for example, had far more in common with those of its Republican predecessors than with the Wilson administration in which Roosevelt himself had served. Despite some divergences, the American administrations before 1920 pursued strikingly similar policies, just as the similarities outweigh the differences in the interwar evolution of a new policy orientation. Of course, the political affiliation of foreign policy makers did matter – the spate of New Dealers who flooded into Washington after 1933 had an impact even in the State Department – and yet most foreign policy decisions were remarkably immune from day-to-day partisan pressures.

Geopolitical analyses, for which foreign economic policy is but a relatively unimportant adjunct to military aims, provide the beginnings of a real explanation. As the international strategic setting forced the United States to secure its Caribbean environs from potential challengers, economic assets and tactics were used as part of this quest for national security. Thus, some argue that as dollar diplomacy helped sweep the Europeans out of the Caribbean the economic component was but a minor sidelight to America's true military goals. It is also asserted that the solicitude with which American policy makers treated the nationalistic Mexicans and Venezuelans in the late 1930s and during the Second World War was a direct result of American concern over German and Japanese influence in the Western Hemisphere; if American oilmen had to be sacrificed to secure the nation's military backyard, this was a small price to pay.

The simplistic geopolitical explanation falls short, for the strategic imperative is essentially indeterminate and undeterminable. In one context fear of external powers led to a tightening of control and a heightening of the importance of economic goals (the Caribbean before the First World War). In another setting an external threat led to a loosening of control and lessening of the importance of economic aims (Mexico in 1938). In a third context, petroleum itself became a strategic good and a prime mover of American policy (the Middle East in the 1940s). We have no way of knowing what role specific security considerations actually played in these instances, and are at even more of a loss when, as in the Morrow Mission, there seems to be little or no geopolitical significance to the events in question. The invocation of the primacy of simple geopolitical concerns seems, all in all, more useful as a justification for policies adopted than as an explanation for their adoption.

A more sophisticated, and more useful, variant of the geopolitical explanation can however be constructed. Recent international relations considerations of the phenomenon of international political hegemony argue that a hegemonic power has an express interest in the stability of the system it dominates, and will be willing to pay a price for systemic stability. This notion has been applied regionally as well, specifically to argue that a regional hegemon will allow more leeway for, and leniency towards, subordinate nations within its region than will a nation whose dominance of an area is in question. In other words, while control of a region is in doubt, each contending power will fight for and hold on to its acquisitions with tenacity and inflexibility; once regional pre-eminence is secure, the hegemon will relax its control in the interest of more peacefully keeping the dominated nations satisfied with their protector.[14]

The American experience does indeed fit this stylized pattern fairly well. From the Spanish-American war until the 1920s, as it fought for leadership in the Caribbean region, the United States used coercive discipline to cement its predominance. Once American hegemony was secure, policy shifted to one of relative benevolence, as the United States attempted to ensure regional support for its aims by persausion and reward rather than by coercion. In other regions, the US position as non-hegemonic challenger in the Middle and Far East led it to use coercion against both rival Great Powers and local rulers to force American influence upon the areas in question. Once America's world-wide hegemony was firm – and along with it American pre-eminence in the Middle and Far East – US policy became more flexible towards and solicitous of both other powers and local elites. In its pre-hegemonic periods, the United States had to marshal its military and economic resources and use them in concerted and concentrated fashion, to open the largest possible breaches and achieve the greatest possible results. With hegemony achieved, the United States could allow for a more diffuse, less direct use of its overwhelming military and economic might; gunboat and dollar diplomacy were replaced by the security umbrella and Bretton Woods.

The usefulness of this framework depends on the assertion that there is a truly qualitative difference between a power with regional hegemony and one without. The unchallenged dominance of a nation's pre-eminence in a particular geographical area is what permits and encourages a radically different, more conciliatory, policy instead of a traditional iron grip. Thus the specification of conditions of regional hegemony is central, and yet it is difficult to distinguish *a priori* between nations that are simply regionally important and those that are hegemonic. Both Germany and Japan in the 1930s were dominant in the spheres they carved out (in ever larger sizes) for themselves, and yet both sensed the challengers on the (near) horizon and used the crudest of disciplines in the regions subject to them. Great Britain was similarly dominant in South America in the century before the First World War and yet *British* presentiments of impending challenge from the Colossus of the North led only to a more or less gracious passing of the baton. The Japanese challenge to Anglo-French control of parts of Asia led sometimes to a tightening, sometimes to a loosening of European colonial discipline; the American challenge led almost everywhere to its loosening.

The hegemonic explanation is also unable to clarify the forces driving changes in foreign policies. The theory might tell us why American policy towards the Caribbean was, in its hegemonic mode, different from its pre-hegemonic pattern, and help define more precisely the motive forces of the new policy, but it does not tell us why the change took place. The approach cannot tell us whether American regional hegemony was inevitable or fortuitous, why British regional hegemony decayed and American arose, and what drove the process forward. In clarifying the political effects of changes in power capabilities, a focus on regional hegemony may be useful; in explaining why changes in the relative distribution of power might take place, it is of little help.

Little in American ideological or partisan-political development is very useful in explaining changing Twentieth-century American policies towards the developing areas. Geopolitical considerations do help describe more rigorously the constraints on American foreign policy, but these constraints are so loose and indeterminate as to be of little use in explaining and predicting American action in the period in question. This brings us to two more economically-based considerations, the ability of local rulers to resist intervention or negotiate a settlement effectively, and the nature of the US economic interests in the developing area in question.

As many have noted, the strength and sovereignty of the local state was a crucial determinant of the costs of gunboat diplomacy to a Great Power. Where authority was divided or questioned, outside intervention against the local state presented few obstacles. When, at the other extreme, the local state was authoritative within its borders, able either to enforce obedience or excite support, foreign invaders faced a far more formidable task. By the same token, the more unified and authoritative local rule was, the more likely it was to be willing and able to engage in serious negotiation. A powerful and/or legitimate local state was both a more formidable potential opponent and a more reliable negotiating partner.

These calculations have two empirically important (if theoretically controversial) economic aspects, both of which have to do with the level of economic development. First, the more developed an area the more powerful and authoritative its state was likely to be. Second, the local prominence of foreign economic interests was inversely related to the level of local economic development. Foreign capitalists in very backward regions were of extraordinary prominence: they had great power relative to local alternatives, and were thus important actors in, and targets of, local politics. Foreign economic interests in more developed areas were generally less obtrusive, and tended to blend into a more general business-community interest. Thus less developed areas were more likely targets of gunboat diplomacy: they were more likely to disintegrate into a chaos that threatened foreign economic interests and less likely to put up meaningful resistance to foreign military intervention.

These factors are especially relevant to our purpose because American policy towards the developing world took its modern form during a time of momentous social, economic, and political change for what we now call the Third World. The period from 1880–1930 saw the emergence of modern socio-economic systems and modern nation states in Latin America and parts of Asia and the Middle East. Economically, these were the years in which significant industrial development began in the Third World. By the late 1920s, most of Latin America had some manufacturing; the larger countries had considerable industries. Truly national economies had been formed out of the disunited, pre- or semi-capitalist, primary-exporting vestiges of Iberian colonialism. In other parts of the world, similar processes were under way. Politically, the structure of State power changed also, not without frequent bloodshed. The Mexican Revolution was the earliest such violent instance of modern nation-building in the developing world. Within a few years China, Turkey, and India were in the throes of similar transformations, albeit in different ways and with varied results. Even where economic development did not lead to violent revolution, major political transformation took place. By the 1930s most of Latin America was involved in the vigorous construction of strong State apparatuses. In 1932 the British mandate over Iraq was terminated and around the same time Ibn Saud was consolidating his rule in what became Saudi Arabia.

The march of national socio-economic and political development in the Third World thus made American military intervention both less feasible and less necessary. Even as stronger national polities raised the costs of the use of force, they also reduced the likelihood of the kinds of unpredictable extra-legal attacks on American property that had often been the excuse for the use of American force. Indeed, the application of the new policy tracks the process of economic and political development fairly well: Mexico and the large South American nations in the 1920s, Venezuela and the Caribbean region in the 1930s, the Middle East only in the 1940s.

Even as the changing nature of Third World societies raised the expected costs of military intervention in defence of private business interests, the very economic changes that underlay the increasing capability of states in the LDCs were also transforming the economic opportunities open to American investors in them. The character of American investments in the developing world indeed underwent an important change in the second and third decades of the century. In 1914, virtually the entirety of American investments in the underdeveloped areas was directly or indirectly tied to primary production for export. Total direct investments in developing areas were $1.3 billion, of which nearly a billion was in Cuba and Mexico, essentially in mining and agriculture. A further $386 million in portfolio investments were outstanding, over three-quarters of it to Cuba and Mexico, again linked to mining and agriculture. By 1929 the picture was far different. Direct investments in Latin America, Africa, and Asia (excluding Japan) were about $4.0 billion. Of this direct investment, 61 per cent ($2.4 billion) was still in primary production. Almost entirely new were the major American investments in manufacturing, sales, and communications and transportation, which accounted for 34 per cent of all US direct investment in the LDCs, a total of nearly $1.4 billion (the remainder was miscellaneous or unclassified). On the portfolio investment side, outstanding American loans to the LDCs totalled $2 billion; new borrowers in South America and Asia together owed about $1.6 billion to Americans.[15]

American economic interests in Africa, Asia, and Latin America had moved away from investments in primary production for export and towards both investments in production for the local market and loans to governments. While the virtual entirety of the $1.7 billion in US direct and portfolio investment in the LDCs in 1914 was directly or indirectly in extractive industries and agriculture, by 1929 about half of the $6 billion in investments was in production for local consumption or loans to local governments. This transformation is of course tied to the economic advance of many LDCs themselves from primary exporters to more rounded national economies. It is of special interest to us because the interests of the latter group of foreign investors were strikingly different from those of earlier investors in primary production.

Foreign investors in mineral extraction and agricultural production for export had few local concerns other than the security of their investment. Markets for the goods produced were overseas, so that host-country economic conditions were of little consequence on the demand side. On the supply side, apart from labour and the resource itself, locally produced inputs were usually unimportant; in some areas even labour was imported.

For the primary-production foreign investor, then, the most important local political variable was the host society's interference in production and export via taxation, regulation, or expropriation. Foreign investors in primary production for export – the standard American overseas investor before the First World War – were thus likely to appeal to their home governments for intervention to forestall host outrages. The authority and sovereignty of the host state was not relevant to the primary investor, and could indeed obstruct him if the local state attempted to control production. Primary investors were prone to form and/or co-operate with private local armies, which could be bribed to protect their investments. Where private armies were insufficient, the home government could be called upon to intervene.

Appeals for American military intervention in the Caribbean indeed came almost entirely from these primary-production investors. Sugar planters in Cuba and the Dominican Republic, banana companies in Central America, oilmen and farmers in Mexico all called insistently for US government intervention, up to and including military force, when local turmoil and/or political opposition endangered their investments. Yet by the 1920s these were not the only American investors in Latin America: primary investors had been joined by investors in industry, commerce, utilities, and government bonds who had divergent interests and different demands.

The newer forms of American investments in developing areas that became common after the First World War were fundamentally tied to the dynamism of the local market and the general solidity of the local political system. The vast majority of the postwar nonprimary direct investments were aimed at satisfying local demand for industrial goods and services. The more rapidly the Argentine and Mexican markets grew, the more attractive it became to locate industries and utilities there, both for general economy-of-scale reasons and for well-known product-cycle reasons. Once established, such American investors were deeply interested in the ability of the local market to expand. Politically, the new investors blended more easily into the local business community and desired, like local businessmen, a stable and favourable political climate and a local government strong enough to ensure this. It was indeed common for Latin American politicians and businessmen in the interwar years to differentiate between 'good' foreign investment, primarily by American industrial firms, and 'bad' foreign investment, primarily by British firms tied to trade in primary products.

American foreign lenders were similarly concerned with local economic and political conditions. Almost all American loans to Latin America, Africa and Asia were to national, state and local governments. The ability of the borrower to repay depended, as it does today, on the general condition of the local economy and on the ability of the debtor government to extract resources from its society and transfer them to creditors. The level of development of the local society, the vigour of the local economy, and the power and authority of the local government all concerned American lenders. Where levels of economic and political development were extremely low such things as customs-house receiverships made borrowers more creditworthy, yet by 1930 such circumstances were uncommon in most of Latin America.

American military intervention was thus of little use in securing the economic interests of the new kind of investors. The Marines could not expand the Colombian market or forestall a Brazilian default: the kinds of surgical strikes and selective interventions that might protect a copper mine or a sugar plantation were meaningless when a firm or bondholder had invested in, so to speak, the economy and/or the government as a whole. In short, the opposition to classical gunboat diplomacy by such a prominent American banker as Dwight Morrow was no fluke. Both the new direct and portfolio investors resented and ridiculed the old-line raw-materials and agricultural interests for their insensitivity to local conditions and their constant calls for American intervention.

The American version of classical imperialism rested, then, upon the firm alliance of strategists bent on forestalling European meddling in politically turbulent backward areas with American investors who required implicit or explicit American government support against local political hazards. The new policy grew out of a gradual but dramatic growth in the ability of local economic and political elites in developing nations to keep order, and the emergence of a new constellation of American economic interests abroad for whom US intervention was neither necessary nor desirable. The two strands of this evolution are obviously intertwined. As the LDCs developed, they became more attractive for both lenders and direct investors interested in the local market. As foreign capital flowed into the local economy in response to local opportunities instead of simply raw materials or cheap labour, the local economy grew and local socio-economic groups in the modern sector of the economy were strengthened.

The expansion of capitalist relations of production in the developing areas, and the rise of new American foreign-investment interests, were thus crucial factors in the transformation of American imperial policy. Of course, geopolitical constraints held, although they were too loose to help explain the kinds of policy changes we are interested in. Furthermore, economic development and the expansion of new kinds of American overseas economic interests did not progress smoothly and evenly around the globe.

The First World War was the catalyst for the shift in policy. The war led to the first great bout of import substitution in the developing world, as normal channels of supply and demand were disrupted, and the march of industrialization that would speed up significantly during the Depression began in earnest. The First World War also dramatically accelerated the expansion of American enterprise and influence into the developing areas. As the war dragged on the European powers pulled back from the developing areas to concentrate their efforts on the European theatre, which gave an obvious opportunity to the United States to fill the resultant geopolitical and economic vacuum.

American military intervention in the Third World did not end with the Good Neighbour Policy, as the sad examples of Guatemala, Cuba, the Dominican Republic, Grenada, and Nicaragua all demonstrate in the post-war Caribbean region alone. Yet our explanations of the reasons for both previous interventions and for the inter-war policy shift give us a framework within which to analyse US relations with the LDCs since then. Intervention is most likely, our discussion would seem to indicate, where geopolitical constraints do not rule it out, where the local society is particularly backward and disorganized, and where American economic interests are either miniscule or are of the old, primary-exporting variety.

The broader implications of our study are clear. Classical colonialist-type policies were the American norm in the pre-1920 era, but had been jettisoned by the 1930s; these two sets of policies responded to different levels of economic development in the LDCs and to the different patterns of US overseas economic interests in the two epochs. If our analysis is accurate and generalizable, colonialist imperialism was a function of a particular stage of economic development in the Third World and of the kinds of metropolitan economic interests that characterized the era. The end of direct colonialism was in turn a function of LDC economic advance and changing patterns of overseas investment and trade by industrial nations. Colonialism was a result of the search for raw materials and agricultural products in pre-capitalist nations; independent LDC nation-states arose as international investment and trade diversified and capitalism progressed in the under-developed areas.

Conclusions

Before the 1920s the United States was a recognizable, if laggard, runner in the race for colonies. By the 1930s the United States was following a new set of policies towards the developing world, one which would be generalized after the Second World War. In the previous instance, American military force went almost hand in hand with American economic penetration. In the latter pattern, the two grew gradually apart, until the notion of US military intervention to protect American loans to Latin America seems nearly unthinkable.

The evolution in policy had three sources. The first was geopolitical: the regional predominance of the United States within the Western Hemisphere removed some of the reasons for armed intervention there. The second was developmental: the formation of modern economies and nation-states in the developing world made intervention less feasible and less necessary. The third was corporate: the kinds of investment made in the developing areas changed from primary production for export, prone to lobbying for intervention, to production for the local market and lending to the local government, neither of which activities lent themselves very well to protection by armed intervention.

The decline of American military intervention in developing areas responded to specific and rationally explicable changes in the strategic environment, in the nature of developing societies, and in the political interests of American overseas investors. A further specification of these causal factors, and their application by analogy or extension to other areas and other eras, seems both possible and profitable.

Notes

1 Cited in Dana G. Munro, *Intervention and Dollar Diplomacy in the Caribbean 1900–1921* (Princeton: Princeton University Press, 1964): 77.
2 ibid.: 113
3 Stephen D. Krasner, *Defending the National Interest: Raw Materials Investments and U.S. Foreign Policy* (Princeton: Princeton University Press, 1978): 355; Leonard M. Fanning, *American Oil Operations Abroad* (New York: McGraw-Hill, 1947): 124, 190–1, 224–45.
4 *Foreign Relations of the United States* (henceforth *FRUS*) 1919, volume I: 873; on the environment see Munro: 426–48. On Mexico, the standard study is Lorenzo Meyer, *Mexico y Estados Unidos en el Conflicto Petrólero (1917–1942)* (Mexico City: Colegio de Mexico, 1968); see also *FRUS 1915*: 870–91; *FRUS 1916*: 741–52; *FRUS 1918*: 687–751; and *FRUS 1920*, III: 200–26. On Venezuela, see Stephen G. Rabe, *The Road to OPEC: United States Relations with Venezuela, 1919–1976* (Austin: University of Texas Press, 1982): 22–42; on Colombia, see Stephen J. Randall, 'The international corporation and American foreign policy: the United States and Colombian petroleum, 1920–1940', *Canadian Journal of History* (August 1974): 179–96. A good general overview is Edward Chester, *United States Oil Policy and Diplomacy* (Westport, Conn.: Greenwood, 1983): 108–207 cover Latin America. The relevant volumes of the multi-tome history of Standard Oil of New Jersey are of course crucial: George Gibb and Evelyn Knowlton, *The Resurgent Years 1911–1927* (New York: Harper and Brothers, 1956); Henrietta Larson, Evelyn Knowlton, and Charles Popple, *New Horizons 1927–1950* (New York: Harper and Row, 1971). See also Mira Wilkins, 'Multinational oil companies in South America in the 1920s', *Business History Review* **48**, 3 (Autumn 1974): 414–46.
5 For production figures, see Fanning: 204–7; on the emergence of less exclusive policies, see Michael Hogan, 'Informal entente: public policy and private management in Anglo-American petroleum affairs, 1918–1924', *Business History Review* **48**, 2 (Summer 1974): 187–205.
6 Cited in Gibb and Knowlton: 262–3; see also John deNovo, 'The movement for an aggressive American oil policy abroad, 1918–1920', *American Historical Review* **61** (July 1956): 854–76, *FRUS 1920* I: 330–70.

7 Harold Nicolson, *Dwight Morrow* (New York: Macmillan, 1935): 264–5.
8 Nicolson: 295; *FRUS 1930*: 462–95. See also N. Stephen Kane, 'Bankers and diplomats: the diplomacy of the Dollar in Mexico, 1921–1924', *Business History Review* **47**, 3 (Autumn 1973): 335–52; and N. Stephen Kane, 'Corporate power and foreign policy: efforts of American oil companies to influence United States relations with Mexico, 1921–1928', *Diplomatic History* **1**, 2 (Spring 1977): 170–98.
9 Chester: 121. See especially, Meyer: 198–264.
10 Fanning: 244–5, 256–9.
11 Rabe: 51–2.
12 ibid.: 64.
13 Irvine Anderson, *Aramco, The United States, and Saudi Arabia* (Princeton: Princeton University Press, 1981): 135–6.
14 On these theoretical approaches, see Robert Keohane, *After Hegemony* (Princeton: Princeton University Press, 1984): 31–46; for a regional application see Stephen D. Krasner, 'Power structures and regional development banks', *International Organization* **35**, 2 (Spring 1981): 303–28.
15 Figures calculated from Cleona Lewis, *America's Stake in International Investments* (Washington: Brookings, 1938): 654–5; and US Department of Commerce, *American Direct Investments in Foreign Countries* (Washington: GPO, 1930): 18–28 and 29–50, *passim*. 'Billion' refers to American billion, i.e. thousand million.

Chapter six

Soviet oil exports between the two world wars

Professor V. A. Shishkin, Institute of History of the USSR, Leningrad

During the entire period between the two world wars Soviet oil exports and, in a wider sense, the oil exporting policy, developed under the influence of two main factors.

The first factor was of an internal character. The state of the country's economy after the October revolution as well as the place and significance of the petroleum industry in the national economy was a decisive factor. It was these things that first and foremost determined the rate of development of Soviet oil exports. The second factor was the international standing of the Soviet Union, particularly its relations with Western oil companies on the issue of the nationalized property of former enterprise owners in Russia as well as the issue of Soviet oil exports on the world market. The world market situation was of no less importance. That is why in this report an attempt has been made to trace the main development stages of the Soviet oil export in the period between two world wars and to assess its condition and place in the overall balance of Soviet foreign trade with regard to the influence of the factors mentioned above.

The first stage (1921–6) may be defined as the years of formation of Soviet oil exports. By the beginning of the 1920s Soviet Russia was in a state of severe economic crisis and dislocation. A gradual process of economic recovery started only in 1921. The war and foreign intervention resulted in a sharp drop in oil output. It was thrown at least three decades back, even in comparison with 1913, the last pre-war year. In 1921 oil output corresponded roughly to that of 1890 (less than 3.8 million tons), being slightly over 40 per cent of the 1913 oil output,[1] although in the pre-revolutionary years the oil production and export level was rather low.

Before the revolution the petroleum industry was technologically backward. Here is what one of the most prominent scientists and organizers of the Soviet petroleum industry, academician I. M. Goubkin, wrote about it:

Bulky, slow and expensive pole drilling, exploitation of wells with antediluvian equipment, predominance of the low efficient steam-engine, a great number of open earthen basins used as oil reservoirs with enormous losses of gas and lighter oil fractions, inability to cope with gushers, predatory exploitation of natural resources, absence of geological service, no work on conservation.[2]

The general state of the petroleum industry naturally affected oil exports. Because of poor industrial development the domestic consumption of oil was very low and the oil share in terms of money in the whole Russian export in 1909–13 amounted to an average of 3.7 per cent per year.[3]

Restoration of the Soviet petroleum industry started in 1921 and initially was carried out on the pre-revolutionary technological basis. However, the 1923/4 production year already marked a turning point. Although the pre-revolutionary oil output quotas had not yet been reached the reconstruction of the petroleum industry began. Owing to the fact that the Soviet government increased investment in the petroleum industry, its speedy recovery became possible. At first the investments were modest because of financial shortages, but in 1924/5 they had already reached 107 million gold roubles comprising 27.7 per cent of all Soviet industrial investments.[4] They had been steadily growing during the next four years. Although the share of oil investment compared with other branches of industry slightly decreased it still remained considerable: 136.0 million roubles in 1925/6 (17.4 per cent); 174.0 million roubles in 1926/7 (15.8 per cent); 206.1 million roubles in 1927/8 (14.1 per cent); 202.7 million roubles in 1928/9 (11.3 per cent).[5]

The policy of stepping up the recovery and reconstruction of the petroleum industry pursued two main goals. First, it was aimed at the quickest possible recovery of the fuel base needed for industry and transport. Second, this policy was caused by the fact that oil was one of the most profitable articles of foreign trade. Hence it was a means of obtaining hard currency for imports of industrial equipment required for the reconstruction of the Soviet national economy.[6]

By 1927 the first substantial changes in the development of the Soviet petroleum industry had taken place. Advanced methods of oil-well operation were widely employed. By this time application of the new rotary method of drilling reached 70 per cent and the use of inefficient methods decreased sharply. In 1927/8 only 10 per cent of oil was extracted by old methods; 57 per cent with the use of deep pumps; and 31 per cent with the use of compressors.[7] As to refining industry it had not yet been modernized.

During 1921−6 oil output almost reached the pre-war level. In 1921 it totalled 3.8 million tons (41 per cent); in 1924, 6.0 million tons (66 per cent); and in 1926, 8.3 million tons (90 per cent), exceeding the pre-war level by more than 10 per cent in 1927.[8] The export of petroleum products and its significance in the overall USSR exports were growing steadily. A low level of domestic consumption partly accounted for that.

Oil exports went up from 951 thousand tons in 1913 to 1.9 million tons in 1926/7 exceeding in 1924/5 the pre-revolutionary export level by 45 per cent and in 1926/7 − three times.[9] The proportion of oil exports in the USSR foreign trade also grew considerably in comparison with the pre-revolutionary years. From 1923/4 to 1926/7 petroleum products were invariably in second or third place among exported goods exceeding 11 per cent of the value of all Soviet exports (against 3.7 per cent before the revolution).[10]

This first success was all the more remarkable, since the formation of the Soviet oil export was going on under difficult conditions of struggle against major Western oil corporations which at first disputed the right of the Soviet state to nationalize oil enterprises of former Russian and foreign owners. Later they followed the road of boycotting and organizing an 'oil blockade' to prevent the sale of Soviet petroleum products on the world market carried out at that time by the USSR Oil syndicate.[11]

The aim of the Soviet oil exporting policy was to prevent any form of Western trusts' control over the sale of Russian petroleum products and to carry out Soviet oil exports and sales independently, getting into contacts with governments and independent firms without excepting, however, the chances of making separate mutually beneficial deals with such big companies as Standard Oil, Royal Dutch Shell and others taking advantage of their competition. That is why despite the boycott on the part of some Western companies more or less normal conditions for Soviet oil exports were secured.[12]

The second stage of the Soviet oil export development (1927−32) was characterized by its rapid growth. Several reasons related to the country's economy were responsible for this phenomenon. First, there was a sharp increase in oil production owing to the basically completed reconstruction of the petroleum industry. The second reason was a steadily growing demand for foreign currency necessary to ensure equipment imports. This equipment was needed to implement the economic reconstruction project stipulated by the programme of socialist transformation including the first five-year plan. Still relatively low domestic consumption of petroleum products was the third reason of this rapid growth.

Further progress was achieved in the reconstruction of the petroleum industry. By 1932 nearly 97 per cent of oil-wells were drilled by the rotary method. The electrification of oilfields was developing rapidly. Several scientific and technological petroleum institutes were established. They began their intensive work.[13] There was a great change for the better in oil refining. In 1927–32 scores of plants and installations were put into operation; an active employment of the cracking process began. In 1931 the amount of refined oil reached 90 per cent of all the oil extracted in comparison with 63 per cent in 1913. At the same time the production of gasoline was considerably increased.[14] During these years two major oil pipelines were put into operation to deliver oil from the oilfields to refining and exporting centres; Baku–Batum and Grozny–Tuapse.

Oil output continuously grew, rising from 8.3 million tons in 1926 to 22.4 million tons – almost a threefold increase.[15] During these years the USSR became the world's second oil producing country after the USA. But as before there was a gap between high rates of growth of oil extraction, refining and transportation, and a relatively low level of domestic consumption. This gap stimulated a rise of oil exports which was bringing in foreign currency still badly needed.

In 1927–32 there was a steady rise of Soviet oil exports. In 1926/7 oil exports amounted only to 1.9 million tons (without crude) reaching 5.6 million tons in 1932, that is 6.5 times the pre-revolutionary level.[16] As for gasoline export, it was 11.7 times the 1913 level. The geography of Soviet oil exports also expanded. Besides traditional European markets Soviet petroleum products were exported to Japan, Korea, China, India, Uruguay, Canada, New Zealand and other countries.[17] By 1932 exports of petroleum products came second in terms of value among other goods. The proportion of this article to the total value of Soviet exports varied from 14 to 16 per cent.[18] The Soviet Union was among the leading exporters of petroleum products occupying in 1933 the fourth place in gasoline exports and the third place in exports of kerosene and lubricating oils.[19]

In the 1930s the Soviet oil exporting policy did not undergo any substantial changes. The Oil Union Export company (Soyuznefte-export), which carried out foreign trade operations, treated Western oil corporations in nearly the same way as its forerunner, The Oil Syndicate (Neftesyndicat), in the mid-1920s, did. Western corporations tried to force Soyuznefteexport to abandon its independent operations. They demanded that Soyuznefteexport should get export quotas and should stick to the prices fixed by the corporations. During this period big deliveries of Soviet oil to some Western firms were made. Soviet oil continued to be a major factor first and foremost on the European market.[20]

By the end of this period the situation in the world market had greatly changed. The world economic crisis of 1929–33 resulted in a sharp decline of energy consumption in capitalist countries. It caused a big slump of oil prices. The world oil price index (1926 = 100) suffered particularly considerable changes: 1931 = 49.4; 1932 = 48.2.[21] This naturally affected the Soviet oil export revenues. In 1930 the sale of 4.4 million tons of petroleum products gave 520 million roubles, whereas, in 1932, 5.6 million tons brought only 348 million roubles.[22] Such a great reduction in profits naturally led to the diminishing of oil exports for obtaining foreign currency.

The third stage of Soviet oil export development (1933–40) was marked by the completion of Soviet national economy reconstruction carried out under conditions of growing international tension.

After 1931 oil production reduced slightly and during two succeeding years did not increase totalling 21.4 million tons in 1932–3.[23] The main reason for that was a substantial decrease in oil output in the Grozny region. By 1940 it came down to 3 million tons against 8 million tons in 1931.[24]

At the same time in the oldest Baku region oil output went up. Before the war a considerable number of new deposits were put into operation there. But the main development was that in the 1930s industrial exploitation of new deposits started in the East of the country, first of all in the Ural-Volga region, in the Tataria, Bashkiria, Kuibyshev districts. This resulted in a certain, though slight, change in the geographic balance of oil production. By 1940, the last pre-war year, the share of the Caucasus oilfields had somewhat diminished, but the Ural-Volga region yielded nearly 12 per cent of oil output.[25] In addition, by the mid-1930s more than half of all the oil was extracted in new regions developed in the Soviet period.[26]

This contributed to a new stable rise in oil output from 24.2 million tons in 1934 to 33 million tons in 1941.[27] By that time the USSR had firmly occupied the second place (after the USA) in oil output, comprising 10.7 per cent of the total world oil output (against 4 per cent in 1920).[28]

In 1933–40 technical level of the petroleum industry continued to rise steadily. At the end of this period an advanced turbine method of drilling was introduced. By the mid-1930s the petroleum industry had completely switched over to the employment of home-made equipment. Scientific research in oil business widened. The share of gasoline and lubricating oils in the structure of oil refining rose higher.

During the years between 1933 and 1940 oil exports began to go down as follows: 1933 – 4.4 million tons; 1934 – 3.8 million tons; 1935 – 3.1 million tons; 1936 – 2.5 million tons; 1937 – 1.8 million tons; 1938 – 1.2 million tons; 1939 – 0.4 million tons; 1940 – 0.8 million tons.[29]

This coincided with a sizeable reduction in Soviet foreign trade (including exports) in comparison with the preceding period. The gross turnover went down from 1.6 billion roubles in 1930 (a record level for the years between the wars) to 485 million roubles in 1940. Correspondingly the peak of exports was also, in 1930, 813 million roubles, while in 1941 it totalled only 78 million roubles.[30]

The main causes of the decline in foreign trade and exports lay in the following. In 1927–32 the Soviet state at the expense of extreme strain of all the country's exporting potentials (including the stepping-up of oil exports) tried to secure maximum flow of foreign currency intended for the reconstruction of the national economy.[31]

In 1917–37 machinery and equipment imports amounted to 4.3 billion roubles. Fifty-seven per cent of this sum or 2.4 billion roubles was spent in the 1929–32 period.[32] However, after 1933 the situation changed. As a result of the economic reconstruction the production of machinery and equipment rose sharply. The share of their imports in relation to domestic production dropped from 19 per cent in 1930 to 2.4 per cent in 1933.[33] Before 1928 the USSR imported over 30 per cent of machinery whereas in 1937 only 1 per cent.[34] As a result, oil exports for obtaining foreign currency, carried out with extreme effort, diminished. But domestic consumption increased greatly and it also affected Soviet exports. Because of international tension the climate of trade and economic relations between the USSR and several capitalist countries deteriorated. It also influenced the development of foreign trade.

The general decline of Soviet foreign trade resulted in the reduction of oil exports. It was also caused by some peculiarities of Soviet economic developments in the 1930s. During this period some sweeping changes in the national economic development occurred; industry was put on a new technical footing and considerably expanded; agriculture was reorganized on the basis of collectivization. Both circumstances led to a rapid growth of oil consumption in industry, agriculture and transport.

As the USSR automobile industry expanded the motor vehicle fleet grew considerably. In 1913 Russia had only 8.8 thousand motor cars; in 1928, 18.7 thousand; in 1933, 117.8 thousand; and in 1938, 760 thousand.[35] In agriculture the number of tractors and combines was also growing at the same rapid pace. The fleet of tractors evaluated in 15 hp engines grew from 2.5 thousand in 1924 to 72 thousand in 1931, to 210 thousand in 1934 and 558 thousand in 1937.[36] The fleet of combines (none of which existed in 1928) already totalled more than 25 thousand vehicles in 1935 and 153.8 thousand in 1938.[37] All this resulted in a sharp growth of domestic oil products consumption.

After construction of major automobile plants gasoline consumption grew considerably: 517 thousand tons in 1932 and 3 million tons in 1940.[38] Substantial changes occurred in kerosene consumption: its use as fuel for tractors and industrial enterprises increased largely. Domestic consumption of oil products grew as follows: in 1928, 7.1 million tons; in 1932, 14.4 million tons; in 1937, 21.2 million tons; and in 1940, 24.6 million tons.[39]

Thus, it was the rapidly growing domestic demand for oil products stimulated by economic recovery that caused the substantial oil exports decline which started in 1933.[40] Besides, the world market situation remained unfavourable throughout the period between two world wars. The price index in the world oil market was as follows (1925 = 100): 1933 – 40.2; 1935 – 32.9; 1937 – 41.7; and 1939 – 37.9.[41]

Nevertheless, during this period the level of oil exports remained relatively high in comparison with other articles of Soviet exports. In 1933–8 oil products were in the second–third place in Soviet exports and comprised nearly 14 per cent of their total value.[42]

In conclusion it is necessary to underline that during the period between the two world wars the development of Soviet oil exports influenced by the Soviet planned economy was primarily determined by the demands of the national economic recovery and expansion and by the needs that arose at different stages of socialist construction.

Notes

1 *USSR Industry, Statistical Reference Book* (Promyshlennost SSSR. Statistichesky sbornik) (Moscow, 1957): 153–4.
2 *USSR Oil Industry* (Neftyanaya promyshlennost SSSR) (Moscow, 1953): 148.
3 *15 Years of Struggle for the USSR Foreign Trade monopoly* (15 let borby za monopoliyu vneshney torgovli SSSR) (Moscow, 1932): 126.
4 Grachevsky, M. N., *Oil in the USSR. Oil Five-Year Plan in 2.5 Years* (Neft v SSSR. Neftyanaya pyatiletka v 2,5 goda) (Moscow, and London, 1932): 51.

5 *Main Points of the USSR Industrial Reconstruction. Essays* (Osnovnye momenty rekonstruktsii promyshlennosti SSSR. Ocherki) (Moscow, 1930): 66.
6 ibid.: 65
7 *USSR Oil Industry in Figures. Statistical Reference Book* (Neftyanaya promyshlennost SSSR v tsyfrah. Kratkiy statistichesky spravochnik) 1920–34 (Moscow and London, 1935): 31.
8 *USSR Industry. Statistical Reference Book*: 153–4.
9 *USSR Oil Industry in Figures*: 89; *USSR Foreign Trade in 1918–1940. Statistical Survey* (Vneshnyaya torgovlya za 1918–1940. Statistichesky obzor) (Moscow, 1960): 45, 67, 94.
10 *USSR in 15 Years. Statistical Data on National Economy* (SSSR za 15 let. Statisticheskie materialy po narodnomu hozyaistvu) (Moscow, 1932): 276–7.
11 Shishkin V. A., 'Formation of the USSR and its Economic Relations with the Capitalist World (1922–1923)' in *Problems of State Building in the First Years of Soviet Power* (Obrazovanie SSSR i economicheskie otnosheniya s kapitalisticheskim mirom v kn.: Problemy gosudarst-vennogo stroitelstva v pervye gody Sovetskoy vlasti) (London, 1973): 266–74.
12 Serebrovsky A. P. *European Oil Trade and Oil Syndicate of the USSR. Results of Five Years of Work on the Development of Soviet Oil Exports* (Evropeyskaya neftyanaya torgovlya i Neftesindikat SSSR. Itogi pyatiletney raboty po razvitiu sovetskogo nefteeksporta) (Moscow, 1927); Foursenko, A. A. *Rockefeller Dynasty*, 2nd edition, revised (London, 1970): 130–54; Sutton, A. C. *Western Technology and Soviet Economic Development* (Stanford, California, 1958): 291.
13 Shashin V. D. *USSR Oil Extracting Industry in 50 Years of Soviet Power. – 'Oil Economy'* (Neftedobyvaushchaya promyshlennost SSSR za 50 let Sovetskoy vlasti. – 'Neftyanoe hozyaistvo') (1967) No. 10: 3; *USSR Oil Industry*: 149, 169, 226.
14 ibid.: 225–32; *USSR and Capitalist World Statistical Reference Book of Economic Indices* (SSSR i kapitalistichesky mir. Statistichesky sbornik technico-economicheskih pokazateley) (Moscow and London, 1934): 64.
15 *USSR Industry* (Promyshlennost SSSR): 153.
16 *USSR Foreign Trade in 1918–1940. Statistical Survey*: 94, 129, 163; *USSR Oil Industry in Figures*: 89.
17 *USSR Oil Industry*: 232, 234.
18 *USSR Foreign Trade* (Vneshnyaya torgovlya SSSR): 182; *50 Years of Soviet Foreign Trade* (50 let Sovetskoy vneshney torgovli) (Moscow, 1967): 284.
19 Bakoulin C. H., Mishoutin D. D. *Foreign Trade Statistics* (Statistica vneshney torgovli) (Moscow, 1940): 308–9.
20 *15 Years of Struggle for the USSR Foreign Trade Monopoly*: 143.
21 *Foreign Trade of Capitalist Countries* (Vneshnyaya torgovlya kapital-isticheskih stran). Statistical Reference Book 1936–1939 (Moscow, 1941): 377.

22 *USSR Foreign Trade in 1918–1940*: 129.
23 *USSR Industry*: 153.
24 *USSR Oil Industry in Figures*: 33; *USSR Oil Industry*: 150.
25 *USSR Oil Industry*: 272; *Oil and Gas Geology* (1964) No. 9: 5.
26 *Oil Economy* (1937) No. 11: 8.
27 *USSR Industry*: 153–4; *USSR Oil Industry*: 149.
28 *Oil Economy* (1964) No. 9–10: 8.
29 *USSR Foreign Trade in 1918–1940. Statistical Survey*: 163, 192.
30 ibid.: 8–9.
31 See: *50 Years of Soviet Foreign Trade*: 42–3.
32 *USSR Foreign Trade. Statistical Survey. 1918–1966* (Moscow, 1967):
    VIII.
33 ibid.: IX.
34 *50 Years of Soviet Foreign Trade*: 49.
35 See: *USSR Oil Industry*: 272; *Socialist Construction of the USSR
    (1933–1938). Statistical review* (Sotsialisticheskoe stroitelstvo SSSR.
    Statištichesky sbornik) (Moscow and London, 1939): 109.
36 *USSR and Capitalist Countries. 1913–1937*: 286.
37 ibid.: IX, 288; *Socialist Construction of the USSR*: 88.
38 *USSR Oil Industry*: 272–3.
39 *USSR Oil Industry*: 273–5.
40 Mishoustin D. D. *Foreign Trade and Industrialization of the USSR*
    (Vneshnyaya torgovlya i industrializatsiya SSSR) (Moscow, 1938) 118;
    International Trade and USSR Foreign Trade (Mezhdunarodnaya
    torgovlya i vneshnyaya torgovlya SSSR) (Moscow, 1941): 393;
    Tugendhat Ch. *Oil: the Biggest Business* (New York, 1968): 244.
41 *Foreign Trade of Capitalist Countries. Statistical Survey, 1936–1939*:
    377.
42 *50 Years of Soviet Foreign Trade*: 284; Trey L. I. *USSR Foreign Trade*
    (Moscow, 1947): 150.

Chapter seven

The US energy crisis of 1920 and the search for new oil supplies

Alan L. Olmstead, Director of the Institute of Governmental Affairs, University of California at Davis
Paul Rhode, a research associate at the Institute of Governmental Affairs, U.C. Davis, and a graduate student in the Department of Economics at Stanford University

In Los Angeles the Sunday headlines told the public what it already knew: 'NO GAS!' Most service stations were closed, and the few still open were clogged by lines blocks long. An eerie calm prevailed as boulevards normally choked by July beach traffic were nearly empty. Business was down. Most alarming were threats to essential services as police bulletins warned that patrols would soon be curtailed for want of fuel. The sole consolation was that the traffic accident rate had plummeted to one-tenth of normal. The gasoline famine that had struck oil-rich Los Angeles with full force two weeks earlier was into its third month in northern California and the Pacific Northwest.[1]

These events occurred more than sixty years ago during a crippling gasoline shortage that rocked the West Coast of the United States in the spring and summer of 1920. Besides offering interesting parallels with the 1970s, an account of the 1920 famine provides a revealing view of the interaction between business enterprises and their social and political environment. The West Coast shortage had national and international repercussions as the area's large integrated companies, headed by Standard Oil of California, restructured their marketing policies and embarked on an aggressive campaign to secure direct control over new oil reserves.

An analysis of the crisis also raises troubling questions about what most economists consider the unambiguous lessons of 1973 and 1979. For a profession notorious for having more opinions than members, the near consensus on the key issues of the recent energy shortages is strikingly out of character. Here the knee-jerk response is so automatic and precise as to make the Radio City Rockettes turn green with envy.

Milton Friedman said it best in a *Newsweek* sermon:

> Why is it that for a century and more before 1971, there were no energy crises, no gasoline shortages, no problems about fuel oil – except during World War II? There is an energy crisis, there are gasoline lines, for one reason and one reason only. Because the government has decreed that there shall be.[2]

The lesson is simple – without government bunglers the oil companies could rely on the price system alone to ration energy. This would end queueing, by allocating fuel to consumers willing to pay the most. According to this reasoning, higher prices are necessary to stimulate exploration and drilling activity in order to increase supplies in the long run.

The troubling aspect of the 1920 crisis is that despite the outward indications of government intervention – lines, rationing to priority users, and quality deterioration – there were no price controls and no government rationing programmes. The major western oil marketers voluntarily suppressed gasoline price advances and instead created a complex set of priority schemes, quotas, and other rationing measures.

Corporate administered pricing policies caused significant deviations from the normal relationship linking gasoline and crude oil prices. While the real price of light crude in California doubled in 1920, the real price of gasoline climbed only 20 per cent. In fact, in the twelve months before the lines first appeared in April 1920, the real price of gasoline fell almost 10 per cent.[3]

Whereas price ceilings normally weaken incentives to produce and invest, the private rationing of 1920 was accompanied by a frenzy of activity to expand supplies. Shaken by the inability to supply its home market, Standard Oil of California (SOCal) led the charge to acquire new reserves. Indeed, R. G. Follis, who would become the company's president and chairman of the board, emphasized that the shortage was responsible for the prevailing attitude in the 1920s that SOCal must expand production in Latin America, the Pacific Basin, and eventually the Middle East to assure sufficient fuel for the West Coast to develop industrially.[4]

This chapter argues that the serious disruptions created by the shortage shocked oil company executives into restructuring their marketing patterns and intensifying their attempts to acquire control over new reserves. The shortage stimulated the West Coast companies to expand the scope of their activities greatly, both domestically and internationally, with a significant impact on the long-run structure of the American oil industry. Before returning to these issues, we provide a background to the extent of the shortage and its political significance on the West Coast.

In 1919 the international petroleum market tightened as oil demand, fired by recovery and post-war business expansion, soared. In the United States, consumption jumped 25 per cent in 1920, outstripping record domestic production, cutting deeply into stocks, doubling crude imports, and driving the real price of crude to levels unmatched over the next fifty years. The victorious Allied powers began to struggle among themselves for control over vital oil reserves and markets. As in the 1970s, dire prophecies about domestic oil supplies gained wide currency. Government and industry experts, anticipating the imminent decline in US oil production, predicted the exhaustion of domestic reserves within a generation.[5] The economic use of alcohol fuels and oil shale was supposedly just around the corner, and warnings of a potential nationwide shortage of gasoline filled the press in 1920.

The West Coast began suffering serious shortages in early April. At this time, SOCal began urging western motorists to 'buy as little gasoline as possible', and soon thereafter, gasoline lines, empty stations, stranded cars, and idled tractors became a common sight in rural areas. As the spot shortages grew quickly into a severe gasoline famine, the major oil companies jointly forged a rationing programme designed to cut consumption in the six western states by 15 per cent. The intent was to redirect fuel from 'pleasure' motorists to essential users, most notably farmers and suppliers of vital services. Government officials played no direct role in developing these policies.[6]

Even with these restrictions, major cities from Seattle in the north to Los Angeles in the south experienced dire interruptions in their fuel supplies. In the Pacific Northwest, motorists endured two-gallon daily rations for several months, and even with such restrictions petrol was often unavailable. The governor of Oregon invoked emergency powers normally reserved for disasters and wartime. In San Francisco, a gunfight erupted in a dispute over ration entitlements, and in Los Angeles, John D. Rockefeller, Jr., had to curtail his vacation because he could not buy petrol! In farming communities the situation was often worse, with many small towns bone-dry for as long as a week at a time.[7]

The shortage caused enormous political problems for gasoline companies as outraged citizens, special interest groups, and politicians declared open season on oilmen. Everywhere, the press claimed that the shortage was contrived, and the Federal Trade Commission and Department of Justice both conducted unfriendly investigations. After initial periods of hostility, these formal inquiries generally supported oilmen's claims that there was a dire shortage of crude.[8]

There is no evidence that the shortage was contrived. Rather, the western firms faced an explosion in demand that they were unable to satisfy with their traditional sources of supply. For reasons that are not fully clear, they chose not to raise prices. At the end of 1919, SOCal's executives anticipated that their sales would increase by 25 per cent over the next year. In fact, sales soared by 50 per cent in the next six months without a significant shift in market shares. Underlying this growing demand was a rapid adoption of internal combustion engines. In 1919 and 1920 the stock of cars and trucks increased 50 per cent, and the number of tractors more than doubled in the Pacific Coast states. During the same period, crude oil output in California grew at less than 3 per cent a year, one-quarter the national average.[9] For the West Coast as a whole, stocks on hand plummeted from a level of about two months' production in early 1918 to less than two weeks' output in early 1920. Nationally the reserve ratio never approached levels as low as those prevailing in California in 1920, but stocks did dip below one month's production twice – in the autumn of 1918 and the autumn of 1920. In both of these instances there was a concerted movement for rationing. In 1918, as part of the war effort, 'Gasless Sundays' were enforced east of the Mississippi, and in 1920 major eastern marketers proposed a national voluntary rationing programme patterned after the West Coast experience.[10]

A striking aspect of the crisis was the absence of price increases during a period of rapid inflation. During the famine, despite persistent accounts of isolated stations selling gasoline for as much as a dollar a gallon, the major oil companies held their prices at 23.5 cents. SOCal and Union Oil aggressively enforced a uniform policy among their retailers, cutting off fuel to those who over-charged or adulterated the product. The majors held firm until late July when prices began inching upwards, reaching an equilibrium by mid-August.[11]

Instead of relying on the price mechanism, the major western companies responded by drastically restructuring their domestic and international marketing patterns. SOCal announced in February 1920 that it would honour all existing commitments, but that henceforth it would not enter into any new export contracts (excepting shipments to American territories). Union Oil, 'feeling it to be a public duty', also ceased exports of refined products. The effect of these policies can be seen in the aggregate data as net exports of gasoline from the West Coast to foreign countries declined from 454,000 barrels in 1919 to 85,000 barrels in 1920.[12]

Even these drastic policies did not satisfy many Californian newspapers and politicians who demanded that the oil companies abrogate existing export contracts and cease all exports, including those destined for Alaska, Hawaii, and even neighbouring states. 'Beggar thy neighbour' policies hit closer to home as local officials demanded more fuel for their constituents at their neighbours' expense. In the farming community of Turlock, California, for example, the Board of Trade demanded that the oil companies cease deliveries to local Japanese farmers. To their credit, the oil companies did not bow to such pressures.[13]

Besides cutting exports, the western marketers for the first time began importing enormous quantities of fuel from Wyoming, Oklahoma, Texas, and Mexico. During the year preceding July 1920, SOCal brought in over 53 million gallons of gasoline to the western states and imported 13 million gallons of Mexican tops. A national freight-car shortage seriously hampered SOCal's import campaign, and as of 30 June 1920, more than 56 million gallons of contracted gasoline remained undelivered for want of transport. As these transportation bottlenecks eased in mid-July, Union and several smaller independents also began substantial importation efforts that continued through 1921. To provide perspective, in the years before 1919 SOCal seldom imported any gasoline, whereas in 1920 its imports exceeded one-third of its total California production.[14]

In addition to stimulating these emergency steps to cut exports and increase imports, the shortage also drove the larger western firms to undertake a world-wide search to bring new supplies under their permanent control. In the spring of 1920 SOCal made an aggressive but unsuccessful bid to take over the Midwest Refining Company, which refined over 85 per cent of Wyoming's crude. SOCal's confidential records leave no doubt that the shortage was directly responsible for this effort. In June 1920, SOCal's President, K. R. Kingsbury, emphasized to John D. Rockefeller, Jr., that 'a shortage of raw material is threatening two-thirds of the area of the present markets of the company. The situation, instead of having improved . . . is growing worse'.

Absorbing Midwest was a risky venture that was sure to invite hostile inquiries and perhaps lawsuits. In the face of these risks, Oscar Sutro, SOCal's legal counsel and an influential director, urged Kingsbury to proceed because the merger was 'vital to the growth of your company, and even the maintenance of its present prestige. . . .' Elsewhere Sutro noted that 'the company needs additional supplies of oil and if it cannot get them in this way must buy other companies or properties in order to satisfy its present market and the needs of the shortage on the Pacific Coast'. Although a last minute pull-out by Midwest scuttled the combination, SOCal did reach long-term agreements with Midwest, guaranteeing deliveries to its eastern territories.[15]

SOCal's bold moves in Wyoming were part of a broader effort to gain access to new crude supplies. After the collapse of the Midwest deal, SOCal turned its attention to acquiring a major interest in the Pacific Oil Company (a recently formed subsidiary of the Southern Pacific Railroad Company). This move would eventually lead to a merger that vastly increased SOCal's reserves. More important for the long run, Pacific had an exceptionally strong geological and exploration division that had pioneered the introduction of scientific methods to oilfield work. Acquiring this expertise had a significant impact on SOCal's subsequent success in finding new oil deposits.[16]

Exploration efforts were intensified within the United States and Mexico. While crude output and drilling of development wells in California languished in 1919 and 1920, wildcatting shot up. The number of wildcat wells drilled in 1920 was double the 1919 level and almost four times the average number drilled in the preceding three years. Exploration efforts were scattered over an unprecedentedly large geographic area, leading to the discovery of immense new fields in the Los Angeles basin.[17]

Union Oil made its first forays into Mexico in 1920 by leasing 16,000 acres. The company's wildcatters immediately struck two gushers that yielded more than 4.5 million barrels by the end of the year. Union's executive credited these wells with saving their Latin American markets, which they had cut off from Californian supplies because of the West Coast crisis. With this new impetus, Union entered Colombia in the following year. Domestically, the shortfall in supplies in 1919 and 1920 led the company to drill its first wells in Texas and Wyoming and to purchase vast oil shale reserves in Colorado as its 'ace in the hole' for long-range insurance against future disruptions.[18]

The shortage also convinced SOCal's leadership that they needed to search farther from home to protect their domestic market. SOCal's rigs operated in the states of Washington, Colorado, and New Mexico. In 1919 and 1920, the company committed itself to serious, systematic exploration abroad. The search began as teams of geologists departed for Central America and the Philippines. In November 1919, SOCal gained from the United Fruit Company exploratory rights to nearly one million acres extending from Guatemala to Colombia. This was added to Standard's option on over half a million acres in northern Panama. Immediate plans included a drilling campaign in Costa Rica, and in the near future prospecting in the Pacific Islands including Australia.[19]

The commitment to search internationally did not lapse when the shortage ended and a period of overproduction began. Between 1920 and 1922 the discovery and development of vast new fields in the Los Angeles basin – Signal Hill, Santa Fe Springs, and Huntington Beach – doubled California's production over a two-year period, causing prices to plummet. Other finds kept supply above local consumption throughout the 1920s. Yet SOCal did not cut back on its international activities. By 1930 the company had completed thirty-seven wells in six foreign countries and conducted exploratory drilling in a dozen more.[20] The company's officials felt that the period of overproduction would eventually pass, requiring new external supplies.

The shortage of 1920 offers insights into understanding the dynamics of business behaviour. The shock created a crisis atmosphere that led oil executives to re-examine their traditional scope of operations and methods of doing business. It broadened SOCal's horizons and set in motion organizational changes that had a permanent impact on the structure of the American Oil Industry. The 1920 crisis was a dramatic episode in the boom-and-bust cycle of oil production. Large supply and demand fluctuations have created several powerful managerial imperatives for oilmen. One imperative is to integrate operations vertically, assuring access to crude oil in times of shortage and guaranteeing larger markets during periods of surplus. Companies also strive to buffer their home markets from large shocks and to stabilize prices. Widely fluctuating prices create political and economic headaches. In addition, managers seek to expand operations, both production and marketing, over a larger geographical area so as not to put all of their companies' eggs into one basket. These managerial imperatives are not always mutually consistent, nor need they be at odds with the pursuit of greater profits or of market power.

SOCal's executives had been burned. They had misjudged the explosion in demand, and they were embarrassed by their inability to supply their traditional customers. Instead of trusting market forces, they devoted substantial organizational resources to protect themselves from being burned again. In the short run this meant holding prices down in the face of enormous market pressures and shipping gasoline from high-priced to low-priced markets. For several months they came close to making water run uphill. Over the intermediate and longer runs, this meant engaging in aggressive merger and exploration campaigns. Once set in motion, these policies continued even after new discoveries fundamentally altered oil market conditions. The company continued its commitment to international exploration and proved receptive to opportunities that others passed by.

Following the fabulously rich discoveries in the Los Angeles basin, SOCal began exploring ways of escaping the confines of the West Coast with highly significant consequences. In 1927, Kingsbury opened negotiations with the Mellon family, which held a dominant interest in Gulf Oil, with the intention of forming a national company. The talks stalled, but as a result of becoming acquainted, SOCal acquired Gulf's concession to drill in Bahrain. This long and complicated story bears retelling here.

In the early 1920s, Major Frank Holmes began negotiations for petroleum concessions with the sheiks of Bahrain and Kuwait and the King of Saudi Arabia. Soon he completed a solid agreement with Bahrain as well as less concrete deals with the other two nations. During the early and mid-1920s, Holmes approached most of the major international oil companies, including Anglo-Persian Oil (now BP), Shell, and Standard of New Jersey (now Exxon), but each shut the door in his face. Finally, in November 1927, Gulf Oil, then a stranger in the Middle East, acquired the leases for Kuwait and Bahrain from Holmes. The terms included a payment of $50,000 as well as an obligation to drill an exploratory well promptly in Bahrain. But within a month the company joined Standard Oil of New Jersey and Standard Oil of New York in barging into the Iraq Petroleum Company. Gulf gained a minority participation in the exploitation of the enormous Kirkuk field in Iraq, but also became subject to the famed Red Line Agreement that restricted its independent activities in the regions of the old Turkish empire. This area included Bahrain but not Kuwait. Gulf then offered the concession to Bahrain to its recent suitor in exchange for a repayment of the $50,000; SOCal jumped at an opportunity that most of the world's leading oil companies had rejected.

SOCal's exploratory teams set to work and found oil in June 1932. This was the first significant discovery on the western side of the Persian Gulf. SOCal then began negotiations for concessions in Saudi Arabia, concessions that eventually led to the formation of the Arab American Oil Company. R. G. Follis, who witnessed these developments as a rising junior executive at SOCal and who later would rule SOCal's vast economic empire as chairman of its board of directors, attributed SOCal's transformation from a regional oil company to an international giant to the unsettling shock of the energy crisis of 1920: 'The shortage of 1920 made Standard Oil [of California] the great international company that it is today'.[21]

There is little doubt that if SOCal had not taken the initiative, other companies eventually would have entered the fields it developed. But this could have dramatically altered the resulting distribution of power in the oil world. If established international giants (such as Standard Oil of New Jersey or Standard Oil of New York) had been first to break into the Saudi fields, it is less likely that they would have found it necessary to split their holdings among several rivals as SOCal did.[22] More significantly, if a British-dominated company had developed these fields, the Anglo-American balance of power in the Middle East would have evolved far differently.

The extensive literature on the Anglo-American rivalry and on the importance of declining oil reserves in the United States on American foreign policy in the 1920s has failed to note that in fact an actual shortage occurred. Hitherto the scarcity hypothesis has rested on inaccurate geological projections and official pronouncements. The existence of a real crisis, with all the disruptions and frustrations experienced in 1973 and 1979, should give added weight to the scarcity hypothesis in the foreign policy debate.[23] Even though the petrol lines were limited to the western states, oil company executives and important politicians in other regions took heed. As mentioned earlier, when oil stocks plummeted in the east, oilmen looked at the rationing programme in the west as a model. In trying to understand these issues, it is important to recognize that organizational changes and policies initiated to solve temporary problems often gain a momentum of their own. The crisis shocked SOCal into intense efforts to acquire new reserves and explore abroad. To accomplish this, the company created new bureaucratic structures that continued their activities long after the proximate causes of their birth had disappeared. It is likely that the real scarcity of petroleum in 1920 set in motion similar bureaucratic forces within the federal government that continued to shape national oil policy throughout the decade.

Notes

We would like to thank A. Fursenko and R. Ferrier for their comments and encouragement. We have benefited from our discussions and correspondence with A. D. Chandler, Jr., M. Friedman, V. Goldberg, P. Lindert, D. McCloskey, J. Pratt, M. Rothstein, J. Shideler, G. Stigler, and G. White. We also want to thank J. Abel of the Union Oil Company and R. G. Follis and W. D. Herrmann of the Chevron Corporation for their assistance.

1 *Los Angeles Examiner*, 12 July 1920; *Los Angeles Times*, 13 July 1920, 19 July 1920; *Venice Evening Vanguard*, 12 July 1920.
2 Milton Friedman, 'Blaming the obstetrician', *Newsweek*, 4 June 1979: 70.

3 Alan L. Olmstead and Paul Rhode, 'Rationing without government, the West Coast gas famine of 1920', *American Economic Review*, **15**, 5 (December 1985): 1049.
4 Interview, R. G. Follis, San Fancisco, Calif., 27 October 1981.
5 United States Geological Survey, *Mineral Resources of the United States, 1921, Part II: Non-Metals* (Washington, D.C.: GPO, 1924): 253–4; *Mineral Resources, 1922, Part II: Non-Metals*: 261–3; Gerald D. Nash, *United States Oil Policy, 1890–1964* (Pittsburgh, Pa.: University of Pittsburgh Press, 1968): 49–71.
6 *San Francisco Chronicle*, 10 April 1920; *Standard Oil Bulletin, July 1920: 7; Los Angeles Times*, 26 May 1920.
7 *Portland News*, 12 May 1920; *San Francisco Chronicle*, 8 July 1920; *Los Angeles Times*, 11 July 1920; 'Extracts from salesmen's special agents' daily reports', July 1920, SOCal Archives, Box 120775, Dublin, Calif.
8 Federal Trade Commission, *Pacific Coast Petroleum Industry, Part I: Production, Ownership, and Profits* (Washington, D.C.: GPO, 1921): 14–15 (hereafter cited as FTC, Pt. I).
9 *Standard Oil Bulletin*, July 1920: 6; Bureau of Foreign and Domestic Commerce, *Commercial Survey of the Pacific Southwest* (Washington, D.C.: GPO, 1930): 358; *Mineral Resources, 1921, Part II*: 260–1, 309; FTC, Pt. I: 71–88.
10 G. R. Hopkins, 'Petroleum refinery statistics, 1916–1925', U.S. Bureau of Mines, Bull. 280 (Washington, D.C.: GPO, 1927): 50–3, 92–5; Harold F. Williamson *et al.*, *The American Petroleum Industry: The Age of Energy, 1899–1959* (Evanston, Ill.: Northwestern University Press, 1963): 285; *Oil and Gas Journal*, 30 July 1920: 2, 60; 20 August 1920: 75.
11 Olmstead and Rhode: 1047–8.
12 Sales Department 'Annual reports, 1891–1922': 31, SOCal Archives, Box 120762, Dublin, Calif.; Union Oil, 'Annual report', December 1920; Bureau of Foreign and Domestic Commerce, *Foreign Commerce and Navigation of the United States* (Washington, D.C.: GPO, 1919–1922).
13 See, for example, *Los Angeles Examiner*, 14 July 1920; SOCal, 'Daily reports', 26 July 1920.
14 In the spring and summer of 1920 SOCal's Traffic Manager, S. G. Casad, searched the country for spare cars, taking 'every tank car I could secure, regardless of the price . . .' (letter, S. G. Casad to H. M. Storey, Vice President, SOCal, 17 September 1920, SOCal Archives, Box 120808, Dublin, Calif.).
15 Kingsbury's statement, in letter, Oscar Sutro to Lewis Cass Ledyard, Esq., Northern Finance Corp., 25 June 1920; memo prepared for K. R. Kingsbury, n.d.; letter, Oscar Sutro to K. R. Kingsbury, 25 June 1920, SOCal Archives, Box 120786, Dublin, Calif.; 'Memo for Mr Barnett', by Oscar Sutro, 27 May 1920, SOCal Archives, Box 120875, Dublin, Calif.
16 Edgar W. Owen, *Trek of the Oil Finders: A History of Exploration for*

Petroleum (Tulsa, Oklahoma: American Association of Petroleum Geologists, 1975): 657–8, 1325, 1328.

17 California State Mining Bureau, *California Oil Fields*, **2**, 1 (July 1925): 11.

18 Union Oil, 'Annual report', December 1920; Earl M. Welty and Frank J. Taylor, *The 76 Bonanza* (Menlo Park, Calif.: Lane Co., 1966): 173–9, 340.

19 Gerald T. White, *Formative Years in the Far West: A History of Standard Oil Company of California and Predecessors through 1919* (New York: Appleton-Century-Crofts, 1962): 558–9; 'Confidential memorandum', Oscar Sutro to K. R. Kingsbury, n.d., SOCal Archives, Box 120786, Dublin, Calif.

20 Roy Lebkicher *et al.*, *Aramco Handbook* (N.p.: Arabian American Oil Co., 1960): 131.

21 ibid.: 117–41; Owen: 1321–4; Wallace E. Pratt, 'The value of business history in the search for oil', in *Oil's First Century*, the staff of *Business History Review* (eds) (Boston: Graduate School of Administration, Harvard University, 1960): 66–7; Follis interview.

22 SOCal, a relatively new player without established international markets or significant political clout, found it advantageous to invite in Texaco in 1936 and Standard Oil of New Jersey and Standard Oil of New York in 1947. Leonard M. Fanning, *Foreign Oil and the Free World* (New York: McGraw-Hill, Inc., 1954): 51–4.

23 John A. DeNovo, 'The movement for an aggressive American oil policy abroad, 1918–1919', *American Historical Review*, **61** (July 1956): 854–76, and *American Interests and Policies in the Middle East, 1900–1939* (Minneapolis, Minn.: University of Minnesota Press, 1963): William Stivers, 'International politics and Iraqi oil, 1918–1928: a study in Anglo-American diplomacy', *Business History Review*, **55**, 4 (Winter, 1981): 517–40.

Chapter eight

Banking and the German oil industry, 1890–1939

Helmut Mejcher, Department of History,
University of Hamburg

Introduction

Although in Germany the oil industry and oil policy have always been closely interwoven with the main structures and dynamics of the world oil market, their specific evolution and performance – in a historical perspective – nevertheless differ markedly from the record of other leading industrial states such as the United States, Britain, France and Italy. In short, Germany, like Japan, has failed both to establish control over an independent oil supply base and to set up a powerful national oil enterprise. The reasons for this failure are complex. The least convincing explanation would be because of the defeats in two world wars, for the other industrial states did not need victories for their specific business achievements. Oil development and oil enterprise including refining requires enormous capital investment. Capital was usually attracted by the prospect of profitable consumer markets. Yet how would finance capital or industrial banks respectively act, when faced with foreign oil trade monopolies, cartels and fierce competition, glutted world oil markets or an energy crunch?

A different set of questions arises from the planning for autarchy, which became the official policy of war-bent Nazi Germany. How would the finance capital accommodate itself to State power and still continue to perform on world markets?

A comparative study of the relationship between banking and the oil industry in both Wilhelmine and Hitlerian Germany is fascinating because of its involvement in both these scenarios successively. Furthermore, the question of continuity can be tested. After all, Hitler's Germany gave the industrial banks involved in oil and petrochemical industries the necessary business security, which before 1914 the Berlin government hesitated to provide indiscriminately .

Yet was the final accommodation of 'Organized Capitalism' to

State power no more than a tactical alliance, to procure an increase of the world market share, if not monopoly control on the national level or in the European hemisphere? Vice versa and seen from the angle of State power, its alliance with the oil business certainly was deemed instrumental for attaining strategic self-sufficiency.

This mutual search for a tactical alliance surely accounts for the meandering of German oil policy, but it hardly explains sufficiently what made German industrial banks before 1914 first interested in the oil business and then the struggle over the issues of state intervention and state monopoly. Therefore a comprehensive analysis of German oil policy must first and foremost look at the structures and conflicts that existed between banking and the oil industry. It is here in the German case that we find important roots for the tactical alliance or joint venture between oil business and State power, which, however, has always foundered on the rocks of world market forces.

The formation and expansion of the German oil industry before 1914: the role of banking and the 'German Petroleum Monopoly Affair'

Oil trade and oil industry: some basic features and structural changes

In Germany oil consumption and the oil industry have from their inception remained heavily dependent on imports. Before 1914 German oil production (i.e. extraction from German territory) amounted to about 2 per cent, 5 per cent and 9.4 per cent of the imports of crude and petroleum products in the years 1890, 1900 and 1913 respectively.[1] In the latter year Germany's crude oil production amounted to 121,000 tons compared with 1,282,184 tons of total imports. Oil was still used mainly for lighting purposes. In 1895 imports of lubricants constituted less than 10 per cent of those of lighting oil. It was only after 1900 that the imports of lubricants, petrol and gasoline grew faster, whereas the imports of lighting oil stagnated. Within 10 years the imports of crude oil quadrupled; imports of petrol, lubricants, etc., increased by about 40 per cent. Motorization in Germany was still on a modest scale. In 1912 vehicles including motor cycles numbered 65,450. Nevertheless, the turn of the century was a watershed for technological progress and the oil industry. Irrespective of the depression years of 1901/2 and 1908/9 prospects of profit-making in the oil trade and oil industry looked bright. Over the years 1900, 1905, 1910 and 1911 the imports of crude oil rose from 8,846 tons in 1900 to 34,373 tons in 1911. Whereas the import figures of lighting oil for those four years stagnated at the level of about 950,000 tons, the imports of petrol, gasoline and other light distillates jumped from 6,167 tons to 9,749 tons to 191,738 tons to 257,203 tons respectively. In the same period the imports of lubricants (Schmieröle) for Germany's new factories and machines doubled from 124,505 tons to 260,455 tons. While the German market for lighting oil was clearly saturated, demands on the energy sector were accelerating.

The turn of the century was also a watershed for the direction of the oil trade, including German imports. Concerning lighting oil, in 1890, American products still amounted to 90.1 per cent of the total German imports. Products of Russian origin stood at 6.6 per cent. Ten years later American imports increasingly had to compete with products from Russia, Austria and Romania. The shrinkage of America's share in German imports of lighting oil to 75.13 per cent in 1913 was, however, less dramatic than the development and diversification of German imports of mineral lubricants (Schmieröle) and of petrol, gasoline etc. The American oil industry and foremost Standard Oil of New Jersey found itself in fierce competition with suppliers from Austria, Romania, Russia and the Dutch Indies, as Table 8.1 demonstrates.

Table 8.1 German imports of mineral lubricants (= L) and of petrol, gasoline and other light distillates (= P) in tons

Countries of origin	1900		1905		1911	
	(L)	*(P)*	*(L)*	*(P)*	*(L)*	*(P)*
Austria	2,243	4,058	6,503	1,313	35,660	54,163
Romania	—	245	—	106	—	38,101
Russia	67,737	96	66,915	31	109,634	22,542
Dutch Indies	—	—	—	677	—	50,840
USA	45,338	1,306	60,422	6,615	111,103	91,146

Source: Compiled from the figures given by U. Brack: op. cit.: 35.

What made the competition so fierce was, that, apart from the Dutch Indies, the supplies from Eastern Europe were largely controlled by Germany's big industrial banks, which had enthusiastically invested in the profitable and rapidly expanding oil industry and energy markets.

The performance of banking towards the oil industry

Parallel with the growing attractions of the profitable oil and energy market in Germany, the turning of banking towards investments in oil enterprise has also to be seen against the background of the staggering increase of banking, or finance capital, in the course and aftermath of the Great Depression. Table 8.2 lists the increase of holdings of the six major German banks.

Table 8.2 Germany's major banks and the increase of their capital holdings in DM million

	1870	*1908*	*1911*
Deutsche Bank	15.0	200	200
Dresdner Bank	9.6	180	200
Disconto Gesellschaft	30.0	170	200
Darmstädter Bank	25.8	154	160
Schaafhausenscher Bankverein	15.6	145	145
Berliner Handelsgesellschaft	16.8	110	110
	112.8	959	1015

Source: Brack: op. cit.: 22.

As banking capital looked for secure profit margins, investments in the seemingly prosperous energy market were a natural choice. However, a crucial decision had to be first taken. Germany's big industrial banks were certainly captivated by the success story of the Standard Oil Company. In the years under survey here, this giant trust had distributed dividends at rates between 30 per cent and 48 per cent annually. In the period from 1900 to 1911 the Standard Oil Company (SOC) had paid its shareholders more than $500 million. In 1909 its net profits of $80 million was more than double the distribution of dividends. However, the German banks did not harbour illusions about the applicability of Standard's system of market and transport monopoly to the diverse national European market. They adopted instead the so-called Nobel system, i.e. the acquisition of an independent and sound production basis with its own sales market in Germany and possibly Europe. Thus the German banks turned to the oil producing areas of Romania, Russia and Austria-Hungary and entered upon a collision course with SOC marketing policy in Germany and in the European area. However the German banks were far from unified in challenging SOC's predominant market position and aggressive policies of market expansion. Their own clashes of interest came to a height over the issue of a German petroleum monopoly. Before discussing the various components, issues and results of this so-called monopoly affair as well as their significance for the interaction between banking and the oil industry, the main structures of the German banks' different oil business interests and affiliations in the south-eastern European regions as well as in the German market must be outlined.

Concerning the involvement of finance capital in the oil industry and oil policy, two main banking groups must be distinguished. They were headed by the Deutsche Bank and the Berliner Disconto Gesellschaft respectively. To the former belonged such middle-sized banks as the Darmstädter Bank, the Mitteldeutsche Kredit-bank, the Nationalbank, the Frankfurter Bankhaus, the Wiener Bankverein and the private bank house of Jacob S. H. Stern. In 1904 they founded the *Deutsche Petroleum Aktiengesellschaft (DPAG)*, a holding company with a share capital of DM 20 million, the majority control of which lay with the Deutsche Bank, which had transferred all its oil interests in Romania, Galicia and Germany (except its Anatolian ones) to the DPAG.

The Disconto Gesellschaft was allied with the Bankhaus S. Bleichröder and in 1905 both banks had founded the Allgemeine Petroleum Industrie-Aktiengesellschaft (APIAG) with a share capital of DM 17 million. The important link of the APIAG with the expanding oil industry in Romania was through the newly formed holding company Concordia (1907), in which it shared capital together with French, Italian and English groups. Other German banks such as the Dresdner Bank and the Schaafhausen-scher Bankverein also invested in oil production in Romania, although on a minor scale. Like the Disconto Gesellschaft they had joined multinational holding companies.

This multinational complexion has implications for the market-ing sector of the oil enterprise. Their German components differed from the Deutsche Bank by being less committed to and less interested in the formation of a German dominated cartel or monopoly on the German oil market. This divergence is well reflected in the short but eventful history of the Deutsche Erdöl-Aktiengesellschaft (DEA), which is dealt within the broader context of the German petroleum monopoly affair.

The issue of a government petroleum monopoly in Germany and its significance for the relationship between banking and the oil industry

Wilhelmine Germany has been called 'Jersey Standard's most pros-perous Eastern hemisphere market' and the petroleum monopoly affair, which came to a head in 1912, has been recorded as 'an explosive episode [which] sent reverberating echoes around the world'.[2] Four major factors were at play in the issue. They merit a brief outline:

1. The German banks were not as successful in their Romanian and Galician oil enterprises as they had hoped. They were faced with problems of marketing their products in Germany as elsewhere in Europe. Although the kerosene (lighting oil) market was reaching a saturation point, it was here the greatest profits lay. But the market was under the effective control of the Deutsch-Amerikanische Petroleum-Gesellschaft (DAPG), which was a subsidiary of the SOC. Under its energetic marketing director Heinrich Riedemann, the DAPG was resolved to maintain its monopoly by all means, including price dumping, and to gain substantial shares in the growing market of lubricants and petrol as well. Indicative of the modest profit margin of the banks' industrial affiliates in the Romanian oil industry is the distribution of dividends. The rates of 8 per cent to 9 per cent in the years 1906 to 1911 compare badly with the 40 per cent distributed annually by the SOC. A further sure indication of the uncertainties of marketing Romanian oil products is the withdrawal of the Schaafhausenscher Bankverein from business there in 1909.
2. As was already mentioned, the two main German banking groups were not unified in their marketing strategies. Their divergencies are perhaps best exemplified by the short history of the Deutsche Erdöl-Aktiengesellschaft (DEA) before 1914. The DEA originated from the union in 1911 of the Deutsche Tiefbohrgesellschaft and the Deutsche Mineralöl-Industrie-Aktiengesellschaft. Both companies had started in oil production in Germany. Because of limited prospects they had extended their activities to Romania and Galicia, in the course of which the Deutsche Bank as well as the Dresdner Bank had gained influence over them. The Disconto Gesellschaft and the Bankhaus Bleichröder had joined in, when the DEA was founded. Shortly after they transferred all their direct holdings in the oil industry to DEA and thereby became the controlling banks. From these mergers had sprung also DEA's connection with OLEX, which was an export-organization of Austrian-Hungarian refineries with a wide network of wholesale firms throughout Germany. Thus DEA had become a fully integrated oil company. On its board of directors ten out of fifteen were bankers. To the dismay of the Deutsche Bank which soon withdrew its representative, Stauss, from the board, DEA was agreeable to negotiating with SOC's subsidiary DAPG a marketing

agreement allotting it 20 per cent of the German market. The agreement provided also for a fixed allocation for OLEX's sales in Europe.

3. The Deutsche Bank, instead, thought, that by entering upon a price war with the DAPG it might not only enforce a revision of an earlier market agreement (1907) between its affiliate, the Europäische Petroleum Union (EPU), and the SOC's subsidiary but eventually also snatch the German market from the SOC and establish its own monopoly control, if necessary by government involvement.

4. One of the preconditions for the realization of this scheme was the security of supplies of crude oil. The Deutsche Bank conducted negotiations with various oil companies, such as the Gulf Oil Corporation and the Pure Oil Company, both from America, and also with the Royal Dutch-Shell. Within the context of these plans of securing a sufficient oil supply base must also be seen the Deutsche Bank's role in the Baghdad Railway concession as well as in the formation of the Turkish Petroleum Company.[3] Last but not least, however, it was the stirrings of political campaigns in Romania to nationalize the oil industry; the penetration of the region by other European financial interests; and finally, the Balkan wars, which convinced the Deutsche Bank that investments were safer under the diplomatic umbrella of a dominant imperial Germany.

The bickering of the various political factions in the imperial parliament (Reichstag) and in the corridors of power need not concern us here. As is well known, the proposal of a government petroleum monopoly was wrecked on the issue of security of supplies. Referring to this, the SOC possessed ample leverage for exerting influence on the government in Berlin, where it could even play off the War Ministry against the Navy Department.

As far as the significance of the monopoly affair for the relationship between banking and the oil industry is concerned, there is obviously no clear-cut determination. The banks themselves were split over the issue. Their lowest common denominator may well have been a growing appreciation that the oil enterprise with its considerable risks and somewhat roughshod manners did not commend itself to the overriding caution of bankers. However, they opted for different directions. The Deutsche Bank called for outright State intervention. By doing so, it might ultimately have been misled by the wrong assumption, that the anti-trust campaign in America against the SOC might play into its hands. The Disconto Gesellschaft and Bleichröder clearly favoured a share basis with other international concerns. It is likely – and of course open to debate – that the respective industrial links of both banking groups played a role as well. The Disconto Gesellschaft and Bleichröder had their roots in the export-orientated heavy industries of the Ruhr Valley, a fact which called for compromise and moderation in matters of trade policy. The Deutsche Bank was linked up chiefly with such innovative industries as petrochemical and electricity plants, which were in need of government sponsoring and of guarantees concerning the supply of raw materials. It may have been not a mere coincidence, that this factor was of considerable significance in our second scenario of events in the 1930s.

Oil industry, capital performance and oil policy under the constraints of Germany's planning for autarchy in the 1930s

Structural changes of Germany's oil industry in the inter-war years

Between the two world wars the oil industry and oil market in Germany underwent fundamental changes. The new structural components can be outlined in the chronological order of the underlying events. For the German banks and their industrial affiliates in south-eastern Europe the outcome of the Anglo-French conference at San Remo in April 1920 was the opposite to what they themselves had tried to acquire in the unilateral – but now obsolete – peace treaties of Bucharest and Brest Litowsk. All foreign possessions were taken away from them and handed over to British, French and Romanian financial groups: The Deutsche Bank's Steaua Romana was shared, half by Romanian capital and half by Anglo-French capital. The firms and refineries controlled by the Disconto Gesellschaft, were taken over by French and Belgian groups. The Deutsche Bank also lost its 25 per cent share in the Turkish Petroleum Company to the French.[4] Deprived of their holdings in Romania and Galicia, German oil enterprise began to concentrate on coal oil, which had been experimented with during the war. An interesting offspring was the merger in 1925 of the two former competitors, DEA and DPAG, under the common name Deutsche Petroleum AG. The old and new rival, of course, was SOC's German subsidiary, the DAPG, led by Riedemann. He was said to have obtained an assurance from the government that no monopoly would be formed in Germany for a ten-year period, and in return he supplied the country with petroleum at a time when supplies were short.[5] Concern about an imminent or future energy crisis, the oil industry having meanwhile distinctly shifted from a kerosene to an energy market, certainly were helpful in paving the way for the entry of the Anglo-Persian Oil Company (APOC) into the German market. OLEX which had associated with APOC in 1926, was gradually absorbed by the latter until it became a wholly-owned subsidiary in 1931.[6] The extension and consolidation of the APOC marketing position in Germany in the late 1920s was part of the application and execution of the 'Achnacarry Agreement' of 1928, by which the three major international oil companies, the SOC, Royal Dutch-Shell and APOC shared their control of over 60 per cent of the domestic market through cartel arrangements for specific oil products as well as oil supplies.[7]

Even more fundamental than this new structural aspect of the oil market and oil industry in Germany was the planning for energy self-sufficiency in the course of the war preparations by Nazi-Germany. Some of its more important aspects concerning banking and the oil industry will be pointed out below.

The impact of capital restriction as well as of geopolitics on Germany's foreign oil policy

In our scenario of pre-1914 imperial Germany, it was explained that the Deutsche Bank, worried or else not fully satisfied with its holdings in south-eastern Europe, extended its activities into the Asiatic regions of the Ottoman Empire. For this it got strategic and diplomatic support from the government in Berlin. In the 1930s, German banking had a new chance to invest capital in ancient Mesopotamia or the newly born state of Iraq. This time finance capital opted for the opposite direction. Nazi Germany's growing designs on eastern and south-eastern Europe promised security, which Anglo-French supremacy in the Middle East, in the event of a European war or a war in the Mediterranean, would make more than doubtful.

The new German venture in Iraq in the shape of the British Oil Development Company (BOD) had started in the days of the Weimar Republic.[8] Ludwig Kastl, Germany's first representative in the permanent Mandates Committee of the League of Nations, with a remarkable career in colonial service and business echelons, had been working assiduously for a new open door to raw materials for German banking and industry. The BOD opened up vistas for a second Baghdad railway era or else for a joint German-Italian majority control. All this happened despite stiff opposition by the British dominated Iraq Petroleum Company (IPC). However, the ministries in Berlin were clearly in a dilemma. On the one hand, the deflationary policies in the wake of the World Economic

Depression barred much needed capital or governmental securities; on the other hand, with Hitler's ascent to power, geopolitics began to leave its imprint on Berlin's considerations. In the event of a European war, with Berlin as an adversary, Mediterranean oil supply lines were regarded as a security risk rather than a strategic asset. The newly won stake in oil exploration in Iraq therefore should be used primarily to procure export orders for Germany's steel industries or otherwise be exchanged against an oil asset in central America, which was deemed safer in the event of a war limited to Europe.[9]

Nevertheless, these alternatives were still controversial within the government. As in Wilhelmine Germany, in the 1930s the Navy Department again pushed the case of securing Middle Eastern oil supplies, if possible at a discount rate. The War Ministry, instead, favoured the planning targets of hydrogenation plants, as they were embedded in the so-called 'Vierjahresplan'. Surely there must ultimately have been a conflict between means and ends. Autarchy combined with imperialistic expansion was seen as a means to provide Nazi Germany with the so-called 'Lebensraum'. Outright Nazi propagandists considered it to be indispensable. Dissenters cautioned against the self-isolation from world economy.[10] It is against the background of this dissent within the Nazi governmental hierarchy that Germany's definitive war aims towards the oil-rich Middle East have remained open to conjecture. Despite all that happened in the early 1940s, it has to be maintained, that in the mid-1930s, Germany, together with its Italian ally, forfeited a new entry into Middle Eastern oil business. Not so in the case of south-eastern Europe.

Banking and oil/petrochemical industry under the alliance between State and cartel

The lessons of the First World War taught the instigators of the Second World War that energy self-sufficiency would henceforth be the key to victory. Nevertheless, the protagonists among the Nazis of autarchy-planning learnt early enough that the production of synthetic motor spirit, despite extraordinary efforts, would fall short of its targets. As the performance of the International Petroleum Cartel (1928) on the German market demonstrates, autarchy on the energy sector certainly was a chimera. Therefore, the Nazi indulgence of the cartel's marketing policy amounted to an 'evil' alliance. More significant, however, is the fact that, under this alliance between State and cartel, banking and oil industry accelerated their mutual penetration process. One of the preconditions was the further concentration of finance capital. Similarly and indeed decisively in this respect was the performance of the State. It fostered a systematic oil exploration on its territory and, by annexation, established new oil ventures in south-eastern Europe. On the other hand, it accepted supply agreements with the 'Achnacarry' companies, which in fact underpinned Germany's dependency on the world market. Above all, however, Nazi rule in Germany allowed banking to reap exorbitant profits from subsidies and protective duties. The Deutsche Bank obviously was one of those to benefit prominently, largely because of its association with the German Dye Trust (I. G. Farben).[11] It clearly shows the Deutsche Bank in the camp of those who opted for a mixture of autarchy and 'limited' German imperialism in south-eastern Europe. Furthermore, in considering the fact that the Deutsche Bank, having meanwhile arisen to the position of a housebank of I. G. Farben, also began to influence and dominate the entire spectrum of the firm's downstream activities, the concentration of finance capital could hardly have been surpassed. Strangely enough, it was the alliance between a state and an international cartel which brought about this concentration of banking power – in the service of politics.

Conclusion

At the close of the period of high industrialization in Germany in the late nineteenth century, banking, which had undergone a considerable concentration process in the wake of the Great Depression, was attracted by the profit opportunities of the oil industry. Germany's big banks dominated oil enterprise in south-eastern Europe. Faced with the forces of the world market and in particular with SOC's monopoly of the kerosene sector in Germany, banking had the choice either to subject to a minority share, or a quota-basis, or else to struggle for paramountcy on an oligopolistic basis. As was shown, banking did not adopt a unified approach. What emerged, instead, was a diversity of development. Furthermore, the problem of the security of supplies made State intervention on behalf of the Deutsche Bank and its search for dominance a controversial issue, which was not resolved, due to the outbreak of the First World War. However, because of the lessons of that war, the oil industry's technological and consumer shift from a kerosene to an energy economy and, finally, Nazi Germany's planning for war, State intervention in the oil and petrochemical industries became the rule. Banking and the Achnacarry companies more or less assiduously subscribed to it. Banking and the oil industry, helped largely by State intervention, underwent a further concentration process. A prime example is the emergence of the Wintershall AG, which superseded DEA in the late 1930s. Besides the Deutsche Bank, it had the backing of the Ruhr Valley industries. Also mention must be made of the Kontinentale Ol AG, which in early 1941 was founded under the auspices of Göring, who was in charge of the 'Four-Year-Plan'. As this holding company was given a monopoly over all oil industries in Nazi-occupied Europe, it combined finance capital, oil industry and imperialist policy in a way unprecedented in Wilhelmine Germany.

Notes

1 Our presentation has greatly profited from the excellent study by: Brack, U.: *Deutsche Erdölpolitik vor 1914* (Hamburg, 1977). The figures are cited therefrom, p. 33.

2 Gibb, G. S. and Knowlton, E. H.: *History of the Standard Oil Company. The Resurgent Years 1911–1927* (New York, 1956): 204.

3 cf. Mejcher, H.: 'Die Bagdadbahn als Instrument deutschen wirtschaftlichen Einflusses im Osmanischen Reich', in *Geschichte und Gesellschaft* (1975) I/4: 447–81.

4 cf. Mejcher, H.: *Imperial Quest for Oil: Iraq 1910–1928* (London, 1976): 111 f. The various attempts by the Deutsche Bank in the interwar years at regaining her pre-1914 oil concession in Iraq were hardly representative of German government oil policy then and therefore need not concern us here. For more information on the Deutsche Bank's various endeavours and support inside the government, see Baumgart, I. and Benneckenstein, H. 'Die mesopotamischen Erdölinteressen der Deutschen Bank (unpublished ms, Weimar, 1986). The paper draws heavily on archival material from the Reichswirtschaftministerium, which is kept in the Staatsarchiv Potsdam. The paper was circulated too late for the Berne conference.

5 *The International Petroleum Cartel.* Staff Report to the U.S. Federal Trade Commission submitted to the Subcommittee on Monopoly of the Select Committee on Small Business, United States Senate (Washington, 1952): 325, FN 97.

6 Ferrier, R. W., *The History of the British Petroleum Company Vol. I: The Developing Years 1901–1932* (Cambridge, 1982): 495.

7 See 5. *The International Petroleum Cartel*: 325; also: Blair, J. M.: *The Control of Oil* (New York, 1976): 64.

8 cf. Mejcher, H.: *Die Politik und das Öl im Nahen Osten. Bd. 1: Der Kampf der Mächte und Konzerne vor dem Zweiten Weltkrieg* (Stuttgart, 1980): 102 ff.

9 cf. Mejcher, H.: 'The international petroleum cartel (1928), Arab and Turkish oil aspirations and German oil policy towards the Middle East on the eve of the Second World War', in Gantzel, K. J. and Mejcher, H. (eds): *Oil, the Middle East, North Africa and the Industrial States*

(Paderborn, 1982): 27–59. Cf. also: Mejcher, H.: 'North Africa in the strategy and politics of the Axis Powers (1936–1943)', in *Cahiers de Tunisie*, Tome XXIX/1981, Numeros 117–118: 629–48.

10 cf. Teichert, E. *Autarkie und Grossraumwirtschaft in Deutschland 1930–1939* (München, 1984): 202 ff. For the illusion of attaining autarchy on the oil energy sector cf. Kasper, H.-H.: 'Die Mineralölpolitik des deutschen Faschismus und der Erdölbergbau in Deutschland 1933 bis 1945', in *Beiträge zur Geschichte der Produktivkräfte, Bd. XI. Freiberger Forschungshefte* (Leipzig, 1976): 25 f.

11 cf. Borkin, J.: *Die unheilige Allianz der I. G. Farben. Eine Interessengemeinschaft im Dritten Reich* (Frankfurt, 1979): 62–74. Also: OMGUS *Ermittlungen gegen die Deutsche Bank — 1946/1947* (Nördlingen, 1985): 116 f.

Chapter nine

The involvement of French banks in the oil industry between the wars: Paribas and its Romanian investments[1]

Professor Philippe Marguerat, University of Neuchatel, Switzerland

In France between the two world wars, oil was controlled to a large extent by the major banks. They ran the main centres of production abroad and played a decisive role in the organization of imports. The case of the Compagnie Française des Pétroles, created in 1924 under the aegis of the State was no exception: this company remained within the sphere of influence of the banks, which were represented among its principal shareholders, and was managed by a team (E. Mercier, J. Mény and R. de Montaigu) which came from the petroleum group of the Banque de Paris et des Pays-Bas (Paribas). Close links were maintained between this team and the bank. The institutions playing the major roles were the Banque de l'Union Parisienne (BUP), prime mover in the importation of Russian oil to France and (together with the Société Générale de Belgique) majority shareholder in La Concordia, a Romanian oil company, and Paribas. This headed an oil empire based on its association with Standard Oil (NJ), in the Standard Franco-Americaine and on its control of two major Romanian producers: Steava Romana – together with Astra Romana, the country's largest company – and Colombia.

The central role played by the major French banking institutions in the oil business is fascinating. Questions pile up: What brought the banks into this area? How did they view their own commitments in this role? Were the assets gained destined for speculations or for investment? Was the intention to take control of oil enterprises and reap the benefits of development, in other words to become entrepreneurs in this business? And this being the case, did they have the means to effect such a transformation, that is to say the financial and above all the technical capacity? All are questions which this study of Paribas' involvement in the Romanian oil industry will endeavour to answer.[2]

Bank intervention by Paribas in Steava Romana and Colombia in 1919–20 was considerable and directed at gaining a controlling interest in the company. But control to what end? It appears that the objective was the 'industry itself'. The bank aimed to use its investment in oil as a tool of industrial management, a tool which would enable it to draw off operating profits from the companies thus controlled. The bank, then, sought to act as a manager in the company, becoming a 'professional' in the oil industry. It must be stressed that this represented a relatively new ambition in that Paribas – in common with the other French banks, had until then concentrated above all on capital investment. It was firmly established in the fields of government security issues and financing new business. While Paribas had in the past acquired interests in industry, this was mainly for portfolio or speculative purposes, thus in a very different context than would be involved in the long-term administration of industrial enterprises.

This then represented a new initiative, explained by the need of the banks in the post-war period to find new outlets. In a diminished financial market, subject to State re-organization and control to meet the needs of reconstruction, access to former markets appeared to be impossible. However several obstacles hindered this new ambition.

First, the financial problem: Steava Romana and Colombia were substantial companies; in 1920 Steava Romana alone was worth FF 400–500 million on the stock exchange, and the take-over of this company would be very costly, at between FF 100 million and FF 150 million.[3] Furthermore, this cost could not easily be passed on to the financial market, which since 1920–1, had shown itself to be relatively hostile to petroleum holdings. In these conditions, it was the bank itself which had to bear the cost of tying up the capital. In an attempt to soften the blow it entered into partnerships, notably with two powerful French industrial groups: Champin, which was linked with the Mirabaud bank and specialized in solderless pipe manufacture, and Mercier (electricity). The three partners brought together the necessary resources within two holding companies: Omnium International de Pétroles, which took care of Colombia; and Steava Française which, in collaboration with an English group, Steava British, took over Steava Romana.[4] But the partnership with Champin and Mercier was not based on an equal relationship. While its two partners, especially Champin, had trouble keeping up and settled for a much smaller role, Paribas was to bear most of the burden.[5]

Right from the beginning, there existed a problem of finance, stemming not from Paribas but from its industrial partners. It is important to remember the bank's reduced power of economic intervention after the First World war. The problem rested in the relative financial weakness of the industrial groups. One might think this would be a passing problem soon corrected by renewed bank intervention, but this was not entirely so. The future of all the oil companies controlled by Paribas would be put under strain by this weakness in the partnership, a strain making itself felt in two ways.

1. The industrial groups had a less important role in the running of the oil companies than had been planned: while representatives of these groups (Champin and Mercier) participated in policy-making on the Boards of Steava Française and Omnium it was the bank which thanks to its lion's share of the total investment, had the last word.

2. The industrial groups had to reduce their fixed assets, which they had originally agreed to do reluctantly and only on con-dition that they would be able to liquify them at the first oppor-tunity. To facilitate this release, it was necessary to market the securities of Steava Française and Omnium. This task needless to say fell to Paribas. However, as we will see, its execution would be in conflict with the purely industrial aspects of oil management and serve to undermine them.

Second, there remained another obstacle to the industrial ambitions of the bank, which I would describe as its 'professional inexperience'. Paribas, at the end of the war – like most of the other French banks – was not really used to industrial manage-ment. It had no industrial section, still less one specialized in oil. The bank had only a few consultant engineers available, who also worked for other clients. The man appointed to head this side of the business at Paribas was not professionally qualified. One of the banks' directors, J. Chevalier came from a career in finance, where he had specialized in transferable securities and Government loans. It is partly for this reason that Paribas had gone into partnership with industrialists to achieve the take-over of Steava Romana and Colombia. It counted on these groups to offset the handicap of its own inexperience. This calculation fell flat. E. Mercier was, strictly speaking, not an industrialist nor an oilman. M. Champin under-stood far better the complexities of industrial management and the problems, not least the technical ones associated with oil. His conception of these mattters was, however, dangerously distorted, being that of a pipe manufacturer who was inclined to regard the oil business from his own particular angle, that of exploration, which was only one aspect, not necessarily the most vital, in developing the industry.[6]

Under these circumstances, the assistance that the industrial partners were able to offer the bank was fraught with problems. All the more so since their financial weakness and status as minority shareholders kept them in a position of inferiority to Paribas. In the case of any disagreement on management matters – and there were many – Paribas could impose its policies whenever it wanted, however well-founded the arguments of its partners might be. Paribas could, of course, count on the expertise of the technicians it had placed at the head of its Romanian oil enterprises: J. Coulon at Colombia and J. Mény at Steava Romana, who were mining engineers, masters of their trade, which was the business of oil extraction. Their presence, however, was not a guarantee of success. Initially, the sphere they had to work in was very limited. It was the management committee at Steava Romana and Omnium – thus in effect Paribas – which laid down the rules for the management of Steava Romana and Colombia. Meny and Coulon therefore, being unrepresented on these committees, were limited to carrying our their instructions.

Additionally and perhaps most importantly, their capabilities as petroleum engineers did not necessarily predispose them to a role in the management of large integrated oil companies. While, they, doubtless, possessed a wealth of experience in overcoming the technical problems of underground working and drilling, the development of oil does not stop there. It rests on achieving a balance between the three main strands of the business: exploration, production and refining. This balance – needing delicate adjustment to suit the circumstances – presupposes a wide range of competence in the necessary fields and demands foresight. One might question, then, whether the qualifications and experience of a mining engineer met these conditions, which were all the more demanding during the inter-war years, which saw enormous upheavals in the theories of oil production and refining with the arrival of unitization and the cracking process.[7]

In brief, an obsessive fear about the creation of a securities market, and the lack of professional experience of the bank, inexperience which neither the alliance with foreign companies in the field nor the creation of branches specializing in oil production were able to compensate for were the two main constraints determining the strategy adopted by Paribas in directing the management of its Romanian oil ventures. What then lay at the centre of this strategy? The introduction and promotion of shares in Steava Française and Omnium on the stock market. This obviously was not the long-term strategy that the bank and its partners sought, but one imposed by circumstances and the precarious finances of those partners. This strategy was also – and this must be stressed – the one that best matched the traditional business activities of Paribas.

The problem remained of how to promote – and then support – the market prices of Steava Française and Omnium. The answer was to push for reflation of Steava Romana on which they relied for support. To achieve this, two main courses of action had to be followed:

1. In a more general context, not specifically related to oil, dividend concessions were made, in other words profits were distributed as widely and often as possible.

2. A second method specific to oil was to boost supply of crude oil by increasing production as quickly as possible. Experience had shown that share prices reflected changes in the volume of crude production.

Management by Paribas of its Romanian oil companies was developed on this basis after 1921. Such a strategy was not beyond reproach, and was to entail harmful consequences for these companies, both financially and industrially.

1. In the field of financial policy, the major consequence was the erosion of self-financing; thus, in the case of Steava Romana, distribution of dividends over the period 1921 to 1926 led to a fall in the average level of self-finance to 50 per cent, which was extremely low. The resulting financial predicament was based on two expedients: first, the issue of shares, and then as the supply of capital injections, which had been over-enthusiastically sought, dried up, the burden of medium and long-term bank loans and debenture debts, which together constituted huge overheads. This was incompatible with the risky nature of the oil business.

2. In the field of industrial policy the major consequence stemmed from the priority given to oil production. This gave rise to a lack of managerial balance as all the effort was concentrated on crude oil production, by way of drilling, while petroleum refining was neglected for lack of finance. This policy was patently absurd, since the equilibrium of the Romanian oil industry relied to a large extent on refining. There were indeed two factors affecting the production costs of Romanian oil which made it difficult to return a profit:

(a) Drilling costs were very high, being subject to the uncertainties of geology and the piecemeal nature of companies' oilfields, which led to stiff competition and the need to drill for oil on an increasing scale to avoid reserves being tapped by neighbouring competitors.

(b) Transport costs and fiscal taxes were considerable.

Because of these conditions it was essential to concentrate on refining in order to secure the high return needed to offset the risks and costs involved in drilling and transport, and still show a profit. As can be seen, Paribas' concern with the marketing of shares in Steava Française and Omnium led to strategies which could only result in its Romanian oil companies becoming high-risk enterprises with low profits. The result was unavoidable: they quickly fell into difficulties, just able to survive but unable to show any return.[8] Paribas' project had failed. This failure was due to a combination of several factors: the necessity and willingness of the bank to come to the aid of its industrial partners; lack of experience in industry in general and oil in particular; and last but not least a tendency to concentrate on marketing shares while ignoring the management of the assets they symbolized. It took Paribas a long time to realize the failure of its strategy. Not until the end of the 1920s did Paribas become aware – and then only after it was spelt out by the British auditors at Steava Romana – of the impasse its policies had led to. This blindness on the part of Paribas was the direct result of its inexperience and that of its partners in the oil industry. When eventually they opened their eyes, it was too late.

Three main options remained:

(a) to abandon Steava Romana and Colombia;
(b) to attempt to re-shape their management; and
(c) to keep the oil companies running while changing the strategy.

The first option appeared ridiculous; the financial loss would be too great. The second appeared logical but met an insurmountable obstacle: little exploitable land remained and, most importantly, few large undivided plots. This problem was insoluble unless unitization was adopted (the rationalizing of oilfields with the integrated development of huge plots of land and the spacing-out of drilling sites) as introduced by the Anglo-Persian Oil Company in Iran, but this presupposed the means to acquire vast areas of exploitable land. This latter applied to the Romanian subsidiaries of the larger oil trusts, Astra Romana (Royal Dutch) and Romano-Americano (Standard Oil), but not to Steava Romana or Colombia, which having exhausted their resources in efforts at production, found themselves, in 1930, in possession of many small piecemeal plots and without the financial means to develop their territory.

There remained the third solution, a change in strategy. This was the only direction left following a decade of policies imposed by Paribas. Renouncing the right to draw operating profits from is petroleum assets, Paribas resolved to take profit on a commercial level. The oil consortiums under its control, Steava Française and Omnium, were transformed into brokers, responsible for selling oil from its Romanian subsidiaries and meanwhile charging sizeable advance commissions on sales.

This change in strategy was to entail complications. While Paribas and its industrial partners were guaranteed a reasonable return from their joint holding companies,[9] the effect was to perpetuate and accentuate the difficulties in which Steava Romana and Colombia were involved. The profit shown by the brokers was directly related to what was sold and this led Paribas to adopt a perverse position with regard to its oil companies. In order to maximize profit through brokerage, it aimed at a maximum production of crude oil, while sales were a priority and carried out even if this meant a financial loss for the Romanian subsidiaries. In these last years of the 1920s then, Paribas moved from a initial genuine desire to manage industry to an attitude, which was regarded by the Romanian industrial community as that of a 'predator'. The result was that Steava Romana and Colombia faced the onset of the Second World War in a desperate condition.[10]

In conclusion, the lure of adventure in oil in France during the inter-war years proved perilous. The organization and state of the financial market condemned banks and industrial enterprises taking part to carry alone the full burden of their investments. The banks obviously possessed the financial means – or at least enough to make a start, enabling them to gain control of powerful industrial assets. This was the case with Paribas in 1920–1 and with BUP in 1923. The question remains whether the means at their disposal would suffice in the long run. In the case of Paribas, when faced with re-establishing Steava Romana and Colombia in the late 1920s the bank drew back at the idea of investing further needed capital. Was this an indication of financial insecurity in an institution unable to guarantee to its industrial assets the funds necessary for development? Not necessarily. The problem was more one of management than lack of finance. Given the right management at Steava Romana and Colombia, the initial investment would probably have been enough to form a basis for continued development. As we know this was not the case. The policies imposed by

Paribas turned out to be misguided, proof of an ignorance and indifference to the realities of the oil business.[11] The consequence was industrial failure, one which bears witness to the difficulties faced by a bank which tried to play the part of 'industrialist' – especially in the context of a newly formed sector[12] which was characterized by strong financial needs and by a complex and rapidly changing technology.

Notes

1 For an overall view of the problem, I refer to my forthcoming work: *Banque et investissement industriel: 'Paribas, Le pétrole roumain et la politique française, 1919–1939'.*
2 My argument is based on the archives at the Banque de Paris et des Pays-Bas.
3 Control of Steava Romana was bought by Paribas from the Deutsche Bank, until then the company's major shareholder.
4 Steava British was essentially composed of the Royal Dutch, Anglo-Iranian and Stern (Merchant) banks. Out of Steava Française and Steava British it was the former group which had most influence – and effectively controlled – Steava Romana.
5 Paribas had 44 per cent of controlling shares in Steava Française, Champin 21 per cent and Mercier 8 per cent.
6 Above all, it must be stressed, in the conditions prevailing in the Romanian oil industry during the 1920s.
7 The problems involved in refining, for example, were outside their abilities. Training at The National School of Mining Engineering, where the teaching was centred on underground engineering, was not very innovative and gave them very technical and administrative skills rather than scientific ones.
8 Financial results, Steava Romana 1921–31 (returns on capital investments: net profit/capital invested – at constant prices):

1921	6.3%	1925	2.5%	1929	0.3%
1922	6.4%	1926	2.0%	1930	0.5%
1923	3.0%	1927	0.4%	1931	– 3.7%
1924	2.5%	1928	0.8%		

These figures can be compared to anticipated returns of around 10 per cent.

9 Financial results, Steava Française 1930–8 (returns on capital investments: net profit/capital invested – at constant prices):

1930	7.1%	1933	6.7%	1936	8.7%
1931	9.4%	1934	8.2%	1937	4.5%
1932	?	1935	5.4%	1938	6.6%

10 Financial results, Steava Romana 1932–9 (returns on capital investments: net profit/capital invested – at constant prices):

1932	1.1%	1935	−0.6%	1938	−1.3%
1933	1.1%	1936	3.3%	1939	2.5%
1934	1.5%	1937	0.9%		

Even then, these figures were obtained at the price of drastic disinvestment, which was effectively a death sentence for Steava Romana (the collapse of gross investment was, calculated with 1921 prices, from a high of about 300 million Romanian lei in 1929 to less than 100 million lei by the start of the Second World War.

At the same time companies such as Astra-Romana and Romano-Americana had, following the slump from 1931–5, achieved more than satisfying results.

11 It would be interesting to study the strategy by the BUP and the Société Générale de Belgique with regard to Concordia and to compare it to that of Paribas.

12 This was new in the sense that until then French companies were not involved in the development of oil.

Chapter ten

The Japanese economy and oil importation

Hiroaki Fukami, Professor of Economics,
Keio University, Tokyo

Introduction

This chapter is an analysis on the subject of the Japanese economy
and oil importation, principally over the period from 1900 to 1973,
the year in which the first oil crisis took place (some considerations
may be made relating to the longer period stretching back to 1868,
the year of the Meiji Restoration).

First, the long-term trends, structural changes and reversals in
primary energy supply as a whole are analysed; later, oil supply is
considered, especially focusing on oil imports.

Instead of confining and concentrating the study within a
specific period, efforts have been exerted to collect and process
data on a uniform and long-term basis, in order to analyse the
whole period subsequent to the Meiji Restoration, and particularly
the period 1900 to 1973. This period can be divided into several
phases according to important changes and differences visible in
the energy supply structure. In this chapter efforts have been
exerted to study on a uniform basis the whole period including the
Meiji era (1868–1912) and the Taisho era (1912–26), for which
period positive analyses have not yet been satisfactorily conducted.

The study of changes in trends over such a long period of time
clearly reveals that, since many fundamental and decisive structural
changes have occurred in Japan during the same period, simple
analogical inferences about past events based on the present
conditions are liable to be greatly mistaken, and are highly likely to
lead to myths and illusions about Japan. Specifically, the fact that
Japan's dependence on external supply in the fiscal year 1973 was
89.9 per cent for primary energy, 77.4 per cent for oil and far in
excess of 90 per cent for industrial raw materials, is liable to lead to
the conclusion that Japan, being a country with the poorest
resources in the world, had depended heavily on external energy
supply even during the process of modernization after the Meiji

116

Restoration. Japan, however, was in fact a net energy-exporting country during the period from the Meiji Restoration (to be exact, from 1879, the first year for which data are available) to 1922 (except for 1883), with the coal industry exporting more than 30 per cent of domestic output on average during the period 1890 to 1905. In respect of Japan's external trade structure, too, exports of primary commodities, if raw silk and copper ingots are included therein, amounted to over 50 per cent of total exports from the Meiji Restoration until approximately 1900, and it was not until the 1910s that primary commodities first accounted for over 50 per cent of Japanese imports. It is an important fact that Japan has formerly been an exporter of primary commodities and an importer of industrial products, up until such time as her recent economic growth had made considerable progress.

Analysis of long-term trends in energy and oil supply in Japan

Overview and periodical phases of development

To begin with, classification into periods is made relating to respective development phases, according to the years when energy revolutions took place. It was in 1902 that the first revolution was achieved, when the percentage of coal in primary energy supply first exceeded that of firewood/charcoal, so that by 1903, coal accounted for more than 50 per cent. The share of coal, expanding year by year, came close to 80 per cent (78.2 per cent) in 1920, and coal continued to be the principal energy source, although its share of total primary energy supply showed a downward trend thereafter.

In fiscal year 1962, the second revolution took place, with the proportion of oil surpassing that of coal, and oil becoming the major energy source in fiscal year 1963. Oil's energy supply share sharply expanded thereafter, reaching a maximum of 77.6 per cent in fiscal year 1973.

The first energy revolution in Japan took place more than ten years behind the corresponding change in the world, where it occurred in the latter half of the 1880s, with coal obtaining a majority share in 1890. However, Japan achieved the second revolution five years ahead of the world, where it was attained in 1967.

Second, Japan, while it had been a net energy-exporting country since the Meiji Restoration as mentioned earlier, turned into a net importer of energy in and after 1923 (except for 1925, 1945 and 1946), and its dependence on imported energy rapidly became

Figure 10.1 Long-term trends of shares of primary energy supply by fuel: 1880–1973 (%)

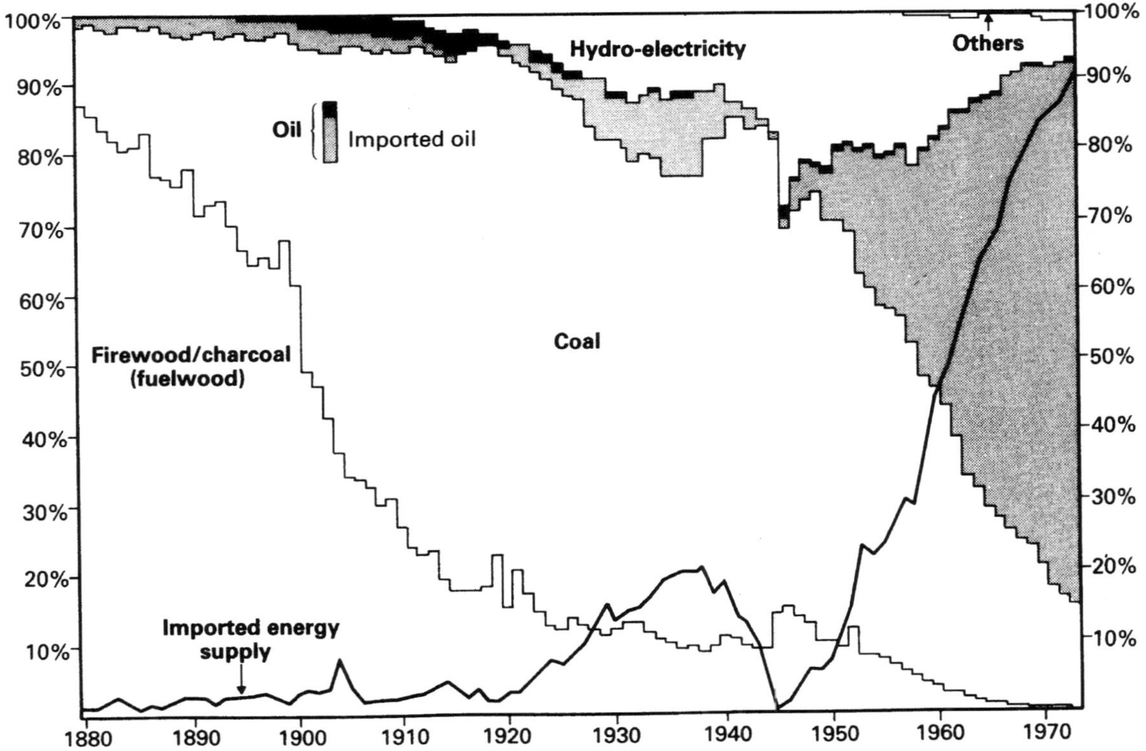

Source: The Institute of Energy Economics, *Energy Economy*, July 1976.

greater in and after 1951, reaching, in fiscal year 1962, the point where the nation relied on imports for the majority of its primary energy supply.

Third, as regards the supply of energy other than oil, coal and firewood/charcoal, water power generation commenced in 1903 and by 1930 its share exceeded 10 per cent, thereafter totalling more than 20 per cent during most of the period after the Second World War until fiscal year 1958. However, after that its share showed a gradual downward trend falling to as low as 4.6 per cent in fiscal year 1973. Moreover, the production of natural gas, commencing in 1914, continued to hold a low share of less than one per cent until fiscal year 1961, when its share exceeded one per cent for the first time. Importation of LNG began in fiscal year 1969, but its share represented only 1.6 per cent by fiscal year 1973. The supply of nuclear power commenced in fiscal year 1966 and its share accounted for only 0.6 per cent in fiscal year 1973. (As for changes in long-term trends in primary energy supply, please refer to Figure 10.1).

Oil supply

Kerosene began to be imported from the USA in 1868 (the first year of Meiji) and first domestic production of crude oil was recorded in 1874. The following three phases can be defined on a broad basis, paying attention to the position and role of oil.

The first phase, 1874 to 1910, represents the age of kerosene, during which kerosene displaced rapeseed oil, the energy source for the conventional *andon* (the square paper-covered lantern), with the demand continuing to expand until 1907, when it began to slacken because of the spread of electric light.

The second phase is the age of fuel for motive power, stretching from 1911 to 1950, during which demand for oil increased, for use as fuel for internal-combustion engines and marine boilers, as well as for military purposes.

The third phase is the age of motive power, heat and raw materials, between 1951 and 1973, with the surge in oil demand leading to overwhelming dependence on imported oil, while consumption of coal dwindled.

The share of oil in the primary energy supply stood at less than 5 per cent during the first phase, and even in the second phase it was only in and after 1928 that the oil demand began to pick up sharply. Its share reached a peak of 12.4 per cent in 1938, but drastically dropped to 2.8 per cent in 1941 as a result of the embargo on oil exports to Japan, enforced by means of the ABCD encirclement of Japan.

Upon entering the third phase, the oil share surged from 10.4 per cent in fiscal year 1951, reaching 51.8 per cent in fiscal year 1963, 60.4 per cent in fiscal year 1966, 70.8 per cent in fiscal year 1970 and finally peaking at 77.6 per cent in fiscal year 1973.

The share of imported oil within the oil supply had been in excess of 90 per cent until the early 1890s, but domestic production began to increase sharply in the late 1890s, amounting to 138,000 kl in 1900, and its share exceeded imports in 1905 (at 52 per cent), and then expanded to 75 per cent in 1915 when output reached a peak of 471,000 kl. Thereafter, however, the domestic production slowed down, and the imports surpassed the local output in 1923, continuing to increase at a fast pace until in 1938 they held a 93.8 per cent share.

During the chaos and rehabilitation period immediately after the Second World War (1946–9), highest-priority production of coal was carried out, and in addition the operation of oil refineries on the Pacific coast was banned by GHQ, thus making domestically-produced coal and water power the major energy supply sources. In 1949, oil refineries on the Pacific coast were authorized to reopen, and in the latter half of 1952 coal mines were affected by a long-term nationwide strike, resulting in increased imports of oil and coal. With this providing momentum, the second energy revolution (that is, the switchover from coal to oil) picked up speed, and the Japanese government began to take measures for the protection and rationalization of the coal industry, imposing customs duties on imported crude and heavy oils in 1955. However, the abundant oil supply at low prices and the advantages of liquid energy continued to accelerate the switchover to heavier dependence on imported oil.

As regards the changes in the form of oil importation, at the early stages principally petroleum products (kerosene) were imported, but by around 1900, about half the imports consisted of crude oil, after which petroleum products again became the principal item of oil imports. After 1922, crude oil began to be imported in large quantities and oil refineries were built on the Pacific coast in 1924, resulting in increased crude oil imports, surpassing the supply of domestically produced oil. After that, the imports of petroleum products regained the major share, with heavy oil and gasoline becoming the principal support items, in place of kerosene.

After the Second World War, in and after 1950, the oil refineries on the Pacific coast were reopened, and furthermore the principle of refining oil at the place of consumption was put into practice for the purpose of saving foreign exchange. As a result, emphasis was placed on importation of crude oil, which accounted for around 90 per cent of total oil imports. Thus, petroleum products were imported only for the purpose of adjusting the supply-demand imbalance, with mainly heavy oil being imported to cover shortages in the domestic market.

It is worthy of note that in the case of Japan, since the government pushed forward measures for high economic growth and for development of heavy and chemical industries after the Second World War in order to catch up with the advanced Western nations, demand concentrated on heavy oil, so that an oversupply of light oil, especially gasoline, prevailed. This shows a completely different consumption pattern from that of the advanced Western countries.

The market shares held by respective petroleum products in 1973 were 55 per cent for heavy oil, 15.3 per cent for naphtha, 11.6 per cent for gasoline, 9.1 per cent for kerosene and 7.1 per cent for diesel oil, which shows the overwhelming importance of heavy oil and small share of gasoline compared with figures for the advanced Western countries, despite the progress in motorization in Japan.

Furthermore, three-quarters of crude oil imports were handled by eight major oil companies, while the Japanese petroleum industry concentrated on the downstream sector of refining and distribution. Arabian Oil Co. Ltd. embarked in 1960 on oil production in the neutral zone between Saudi Arabia and Kuwait, which was the first overseas development project undertaken by Japanese oil developers after the Second World War. Thereafter, in 1964, the Japan National Oil Corporation was established, to engage primarily in investing and lending for overseas exploration activities. The supply share of Japanese oil developers, however, stands at only 8 to 10 per cent.

When making a broad review of Japan's economic development, especially of the growth after the Second World War, it is noticeable that Japan has made the most of the potential advantages of relative backwardness, as pointed out by A. Gerschenkrom. The Japanese petroleum industry can also be said to have had an advantage in that while depending largely on simple imports for oil supply, it introduced up-to-date technology and established modern oil refining facilities after the war, being free of the constraints imposed by out-dated facilities (destroyed during the war).

Another fact worthy of attention is that the geographical features of Japan as a maritime power have been utilized effectively, by using large-sized oil carriers for rationalization and cost saving in oil transportation, coupled with the development of coastal industrial zones helped by good natural harbours.

Japan's economic development and supply-demand conditions for energy and coal

Long-term trends in supply and demand per capita

Energy consumption (or supply) per capital is considered as one of the indicators for measuring a country's economic growth and the living standard of the people.

The long-term respective changes in primary energy consumption, oil consumption and amount of imported oil (all per capita) are shown as follows (see Figure 10.2): for 1880, 156.8 kg (expressed as coal equivalent, using a basis of 7,000 kcal/kg – this figure is used throughout, 2.2 kg, 2.0 kg; for 1900, 229.1 kg, 11.9 kg, 7.4 kg; for 1940, 1,154.7 kg, 88.7 kg, 82.1 kg. The primary energy consumption in 1940 marked the pre-war peak. (Oil consumption and oil imports per capita peaked in 1938 at 126.1 kg and 118.3 kg respectively.) (Since long-term data on energy consumption are unavailable, figures on primary energy supply are used here, excluding coal exports for the period to the end of the Second World War.)

In 1945, as the Second World War came to an end, the respective consumptions per capita sharply decreased to 550.9 kg, 5.0 kg and 0.2 kg, but recovered in 1950 to 829.8 kg, 51.9 kg and 46.2 kg. Primary energy consumption exceeded the pre-war peak in fiscal year 1959 while oil consumption and oil imports rose above the highest pre-war level in fiscal year 1953. In fiscal year 1973, these three items reached their highest levels of 5,009.1 kg, 3,888.7 kg and 3,878.6 kg respectively, approaching rapidly the levels of Western countries.

Annual rates of consumption (supply) increase per head of the population are presented in Table 10.1. The consumption (supply) continued to increase at a surprisingly high rate, except for the chaotic period during and immediately after the Second World War, and the pace accelerated still further after the war, with oil consumption in particular continuing to climb at an annual rate of a little more than 20 per cent.

Consumption per unit of GNP and GNP elasticity of energy supply

In order to look into the direct relationships between economic growth and supply of energy and oil, a discussion follows of the

Figure 10.2 Long-term trends of primary energy supply, oil supply and imported oil per capita (kg coal equivalent)

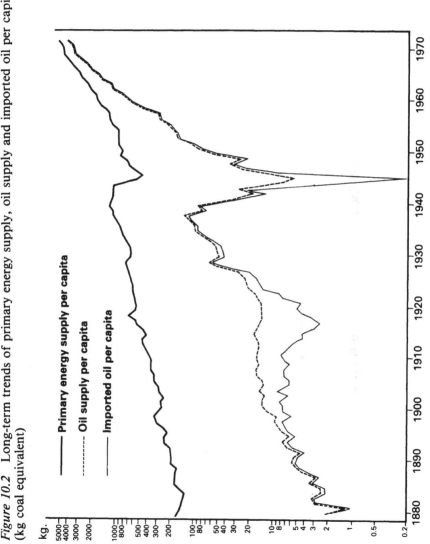

Figure 10.3 Long-term trends of primary energy supply, oil supply and imported oil per GNP unit
(kg coal equivalent)

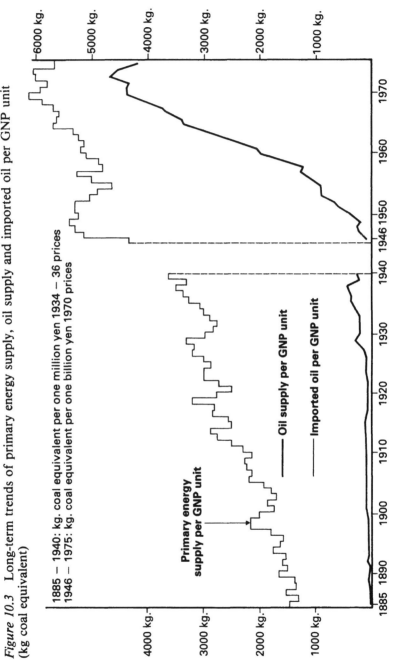

1885 – 1940: kg. coal equivalent per one million yen 1934 – 36 prices
1946 – 1975: kg. coal equivalent per one billion yen 1970 prices

Primary energy
supply per GNP unit

Oil supply per GNP unit

Imported oil per GNP unit

Table 10.1 Average annual rate of increase of per capita supply

	Primary energy supply per capita (%)	Oil supply per capita (%)	Oil import per capita (%)
1880–1973	3.80	8.37	8.48
1880–1900	3.06	4.69	6.76
1900–1973	4.00	8.25	8.96
1900–1938	3.39	6.41	7.57
1950–1973	8.13	20.64	21.24
1950–1960	5.62	26.41	27.68
1960–1970	11.55	18.79	18.95
1970–1973	5.42	8.71	8.76

Table 10.2 Average annual rate of increase of energy supply, GNP and industrial production

	Primary energy supply (%)	Primary energy import (%)	Oil supply (%)	Oil import (%)	Industrial production (%)	GNP (%)
1880–1973	5.02 <0.85>	9.64 <1.63>	9.68 <1.63>	9.78 <1.65>	5.93	1890–1973 4.15
1880–1900	3.99 <0.90>	4.27 <0.96>	9.91 <2.23>	7.84 <1.77>	4.44	1890–1900 5.59
1900–1973	5.30 (1.34) <0.84>	10.14 (2.56) <1.60>	9.61 (2.43) <1.52>	10.32 (2.61) <1.63>	6.33	3.96
1900–1938	4.71 (1.47) <0.63>	9.87 (3.07) <1.32>	7.76 (2.42) <1.04>	8.93 (2.78) <1.20>	7.45	3.21
1950–1973	10.16 (1.07) <0.73>	22.43 (2.37) <1.61>	22.08 (2.33) <1.58>	22.68 (2.39) <1.62>	13.96	9.48
1950–1960	8.54 (0.97) <0.53>	28.90 (3.28) <1.80>	27.89 (3.17) <1.73>	29.16 (3.31) <1.81>	16.09	8.80
1960–1970	12.72 (1.19) <0.94>	20.12 (1.89) <1.48>	20.04 (1.88) <1.48>	20.20 (1.89) <1.49>	13.58	10.67
1970–1973	7.21 (0.92) <1.00>	9.87 (1.26) <1.37>	10.56 (1.35) <1.46>	10.61 (1.36) <1.47>	7.23	7.82

(   ) = GNP elasticity of energy supply.
<   > = Industrial production elasticity of energy supply.

long-term movements in the consumption (supply) of primary energy, petroleum and imported oil per GNP unit. (Since it is difficult to obtain a linking index accurate for both pre-war and post-war periods for calculation of real GNP, the pre-war unit consumption (supply) is expressed in kg per million yen based on 1934–6 prices and the post-war unit consumption is in kg per billion yen based on 1970 prices.)

As indicated in Figure 10.3, although consumption or supply of energy per unit of GNP displayed an upward tendency, and rose sharply during the period of progressive heavy and chemical industry development, the rise in supply per unit of GNP during the post-war high growth period was in fact more moderate than it was in the pre-war years, as a result of improved utilization efficiency, which was achieved through the energy revolution. However, supply of petroleum and imported oil per unit of GNP sharply increased after the war by factors of 12.3 and 13.7 respectively during the 1950–73 period, as against the moderate rise of 15.3 per cent in supply of primary energy, highlighting the drastic changes in energy sources.

In addition, with a view to further clarifying the relationships between economic growth and energy/oil supply, long-term growth rates of GNP, industrial production, primary energy supply/imports and oil supply/imports have been evaluated to calculate the respective GNP elasticities and industrial production elasticities. As compiled in Table 10.2, the respective elasticities of oil supply and oil imports are in excess of one for the whole period under review, while the industrial production elasticities of primary energy supply are below one, and that of GNP above one, except for the 1950s and the 1970–3 period. This clearly indicates that Japan's dependence on oil continued to grow steadily all through the process of its modern economic growth and industrialization, with even heavier recourse to imported oil, that is to say, imported energy.

Oil imports and import prices

Despite the growing dependence on imported energy, and on imported oil in particular, Japan's energy imports accounted for only 2 to 5 per cent of her total imports till the end of the 1920s, reaching the peak of 7.4 per cent in the 1930s. After the war, this share steadily expanded, recording 11 per cent in the first half of the 1950s, 15.7 per cent in the latter half, 18.3 per cent in the first half of the 1960s and 20.4 per cent in the latter half. Oil imports, meanwhile, held a share of 11.6 per cent in the latter half of the

126

1950s, 14.2 per cent in the first half of the 1960s, 15.8 per cent in the latter half of the 1960s, 17.6 per cent in 1973 and then sharply increased their share to 34.1 per cent in 1974 and 36.3 per cent in 1975, when they were hard hit by the first oil crisis.

Import prices (CIF) of crude oil continued to decline in and after fiscal year 1957 from $3.40/barrel down to $1.89/barrel in fiscal year 1966, $1.94 in fiscal year 1967, $1.88 in fiscal year 1968 and $1.80 in fiscal year 1969, the lowest ever price. Import prices then began an upward trend, rising to $1.83 in fiscal year 1970, $2.30 in fiscal year 1971, $2.57 in fiscal year 1972, $4.85 in fiscal year 1973, $11.52 in fiscal year 1974 and $12.06 in fiscal year 1975. These low import prices greatly encouraged the switchover to imported oil, and also contributed to the high post-war economic growth of Japan. The sharp upturn in the share of oil imports in the nation's total imports, which occurred despite a fall in prices, indicates how rapidly and sharply the oil imports increased during this period.

Conclusion

In the present study, analysis has focused on the long-term general trends and structural changes. Japan depended more and more on imported energy, especially oil, throughout the course of the post-war high-growth period. From the purely economic point of view, this was indeed a very reasonable strategy, and were it not for such a changeover in energy sources, Japan's high economic growth and great improvement in living standards would have been impossible, under the constraints of limited supply and high prices of domestically produced energy.

However, Japan's extremely high reliance on imported energy/oil resulted in a critical impact and blow to the Japanese economy after the outbreak of the first oil crisis in October 1973. In fiscal year 1974, Japan recorded a negative growth rate for the first time after the war, suffering a trilemma – inflation, unemployment/recession and deficits in the balance of payments. Under such serious circumstances, it was hotly debated at that time whether the emphasis should be shifted to a policy of ensuring economic security or stability, which had been neglected since the war.

In the course of over ten years since that time, Japan has succeeded in overcoming the trilemma, displaying an outstanding adaptability; at the same time, while endeavouring to ensure effective utilization and conservation of energy/oil, Japan made rapid progress in changing oil to alternative energy sources. Consequently, the emphasis of policy has also shifted towards the theory of the ideal or best mix, aiming at compatibility and simultaneous attainment of security of supply and economy of cost.

History, while underlining the importance of world peace and international harmony, seems to be telling us that it is essential to maintain and strengthen our capacity for economic adjustment and transformation.

Japan, at this juncture, should alter her former passive policy of response, merely relying on her outstanding ability to adapt to changes in the international situation, particularly in the international economic and energy situation, and should now make some positive approaches to international economic and energy problems, in order to contribute to the improvement of the situation, in a manner favourable to the whole world as well as to Japan.

For reasons of space, detailed and in-depth analysis regarding the relationships between oil imports and changes in industrial structure, and so on, for respective phases and periods has had to be omitted.

Index

Muhammad Riza Shah 22
Musaddiq, Dr Muhammad 24, 38

Naftesyndicat 77
National Iranian Oil Company,
  N.I.O.C. 21, 22, 24–7
New Zealand 77
Nicaragua 54, 70
Nicholson, Meredith 60, 61
Nixon, President Richard 41
North Sea 44
Norway 46

Oil and Gas Journal 39
Oil Producing Export Countries,
  OPEC 13, 14, 20, 43–7
Oil Syndicate of the USSR 76
Oklahoma 87
OLEX 99, 100, 102
Omnium International de Pétroles
  108–13
Ottoman Empire, Government 7,
  57, 102

Palestine 57
Panama 54, 56, 88
Paraguay 30, 31
Persian Gulf 12, 42, 43, 46, 61,
  62, 90
Peru 28–31, 56
Petroleas Mexicanas, Pemex 18
Petroleo Brasileiro, Petrobas 18,
  33, 34
Petromin 21, 22, 25–7
Philippines, The 54, 88
Puerto Rico 54
Pure Oil Company 100

Reagan, President Ronald 39
Riedmann, Heinrich 99, 101
Rockefeller, John D. 85, 87
Romania 38, 57, 96, 98–101, 107,
  110–13
Romano-Americano 112
Roosevelt Corollary 53
Rotterdam 45

Royal Dutch-Shell Company 4–8,
  19, 29, 44, 56, 57, 76, 100, 102

San Remo Conference 101
Saudi Arabia 6, 8–10, 13, 14, 21,
  22, 25, 45, 67, 90, 121
South America 28–30, 34, 65, 67
Soviet Union (Russia) and
  Russians 3, 4, 38–40, 47, 55,
  74–80, 96, 107
Soyuznaft-export 77, 78
Standard Franco-Americaine 107
Standard Oil Company of Indiana
  7
Steava Romana 107–11

Tataria, Bashkiria, Kuidyshev
  Region 78
Texas 87
Texas Oil Company 5, 6, 8, 19
Trinidad 28
Turkey 67

Union Oil Company 86–8
United Kingdom (Great Britain) 5,
  9, 24, 44, 46, 54–8, 65, 67, 91,
  94, 101
United States (America) 3–6,
  11–13, 15, 24, 38, 39, 41–5,
  53–72, 77, 78, 83–5, 91, 94, 96,
  100, 119
Uruguay 30, 31, 77
Ural-Volga region 78

Vargas, President Getulio 32
Venezuela and Government 6–8,
  10, 28–31, 55, 56, 60–3, 67

West, the 37, 38, 41, 43, 44, 46,
  47, 76, 78, 121
West Coast, USA 83–8, 90
Wintershall Allgemeinschaft 105
Wyoming 87, 88

Yacimientos Petroliferos Fiscales,
  YPF 18, 30